W9-AZS-768

HISTORY OF CRIME AND PUNISHMENT

THE US PRISON SYSTEM AND PRISON LIFE

BY DUCHESS HARRIS, JD, PHD
WITH KATE CONLEY

Essential Library

An Imprint of Abdo Publishing | abdobooks.com

ABDOBOOKS.COM

Published by Abdo Publishing, a division of ABDO, PO Box 398166, Minneapolis, Minnesota 55439. Copyright © 2020 by Abdo Consulting Group, Inc. International copyrights reserved in all countries. No part of this book may be reproduced in any form without written permission from the publisher. Essential Library™ is a trademark and logo of Abdo Publishing.

Printed in the United States of America, North Mankato, Minnesota.
042019
092019

Interior Photos: Ted S. Warren/AP Images, 5; Rainmaker Photo/MediaPunch/IPX/AP Images, 9; Mark Bonifacio/New York Daily News Archive/New York Daily News/Getty Images, 12; Jack Rice/AP Images, 15; North Wind Picture Archives, 16; Jesse Dearing/The Boston Globe/Getty Images, 22, 59, 75; Adam McCaw/Independent Record/AP Images, 25; AP Images, 27, 28; Rich Pedroncelli/AP Images, 33, 63, 94; George Rose/Getty Images News/Getty Images, 35; Richard Shotwell/Invision/AP, 37; David Tran Photo/Shutterstock Images, 39; Seth Wenig/AP Images, 41; Jeffrey Collins/AP Images, 45; Andrew D. Brosig/The Daily Sentinel/AP Images, 46; Andrew Harnik/AP Images, 49; Melissa Phillip/Houston Chronicle/AP Images, 50; Shaul Schwarz/Reportage Archive/Getty Images, 55; David Goldman/AP Images, 60; Andy Cross/The Denver Post/Getty Images, 64, 86; Noah Berger/Bloomberg/Getty Images, 69; Alex Hicks/Spartanburg Herald-Journal/AP Images, 70; Joe Kline/The Bulletin/AP Images, 79; Al Hartmann/The Salt Lake Tribune/AP Images, 80; Yoon S. Byun/The Boston Globe/Getty Images, 88; Cinthia Ritchie/Chugiak Eagle River Star/AP Images, 91

Editor: Charly Haley
Series Designer: Dan Peluso

LIBRARY OF CONGRESS CONTROL NUMBER: 2018965971

PUBLISHER'S CATALOGING-IN-PUBLICATION DATA

Names: Harris, Duchess, author | Conley, Kate, author.
Title: The US prison system and prison life / by Duchess Harris and Kate Conley
Description: Minneapolis, Minnesota: Abdo Publishing, 2020 | Series: History of crime and punishment | Includes online resources and index.
Identifiers: ISBN 9781532119224 (lib. bdg.) | ISBN 9781532173400 (ebook)
Subjects: LCSH: Prisons--United States--Juvenile literature. | Correctional institutions--Inmates--Juvenile literature. | Prison sentences--United States--Juvenile literature. | Prisoners and prisons--Juvenile literature.
Classification: DDC 365.973--dc23

CONTENTS

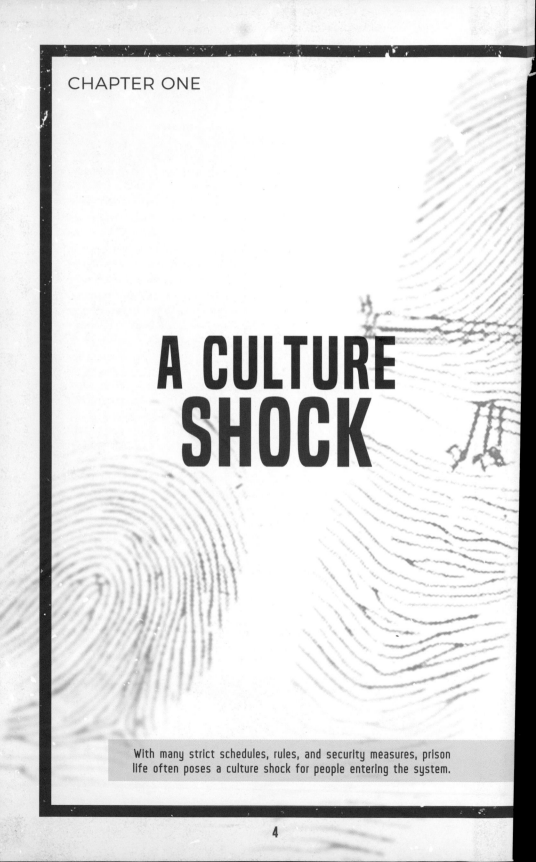

CHAPTER ONE

A CULTURE SHOCK

With many strict schedules, rules, and security measures, prison life often poses a culture shock for people entering the system.

"**A**t first, I was in denial. I was thinking, 'No. There's no way they're going to give me a life sentence at 21,'" recalled an inmate at California's San Quentin State Prison. "[But then] the judge slammed the gavel down and said, 'I'm sentencing you to life in prison.' And I was just like, 'Wow.' It just totally dumbfounded me."[1]

Prison is a reality for thousands of people each year. People who have been convicted of a crime and sentenced to prison time face immense lifestyle changes. They must leave behind their family, friends, jobs, and overall freedom. It's a culture shock, especially for people entering prison for the first time. A prison has its own social order, attitudes, slang language, and rules.

Prison life is often shrouded in Hollywood myths and inaccurate information. Another San Quentin inmate, Earlonne Woods, wanted to change that. Woods spent 21 years in prison after driving the getaway car in an attempted robbery. In 2016, while still in prison, Woods teamed up with Nigel Poor, an artist who volunteers at San Quentin, to set the record straight on prison life. Woods and Poor are the cohosts of *Ear Hustle*. It is the first podcast ever created inside a state or federal prison. It tells stories through interviews with San Quentin inmates.

The podcast takes its name from the prison slang term *ear hustle*, which means to eavesdrop. And that is precisely what the podcast allows listeners to do. It captures a variety of topics, from cellmates to solitary confinement. *Ear Hustle* is raw and unfiltered. Its stories display the hope, boredom, and despair of prison life that people outside of prison walls rarely hear.

PRISONS TODAY

The *Ear Hustle* podcast has drawn attention to problems in the vast US prison system. The United States has the world's highest rate of incarceration. For every 100,000 Americans, 655 are behind bars.[2] The United States held 22 percent of the world's prisoners as of 2011, despite the fact that the country only had approximately 4.4 percent of the world's population.[3]

The spike in incarceration rates began in the 1970s. At that time, rising crime levels led to public outcry. In response, state

SAN QUENTIN

San Quentin is California's oldest state prison. Its roots stretch back to the California gold rush. Between 1848 and 1852, approximately 300,000 people moved to California in search of gold. The increase in California's population was followed by an increase in crime. Local jails ran out of space, and convicts were locked up on ships in San Francisco Bay. San Quentin opened in 1854 with room for 250 inmates. Since that time, San Quentin has grown into a massive facility. By 2018, it housed nearly 4,000 inmates.[4]

THE CRIMINAL JUSTICE SYSTEM

Several agencies within federal, state, and local governments have the power to uphold laws. These agencies are collectively known as the criminal justice system. The criminal justice system includes police officers, judges, lawyers, correctional officers, parole authorities, and prisons. In 2018, the US criminal justice system oversaw almost seven million people.[7] This number included people in jails and prisons as well as people on parole or probation.

and federal leaders changed sentencing guidelines. New policies created mandatory minimum sentencing guidelines. This decreased judges' flexibility in how long they sentenced a convicted offender to prison. For example, under federal law, a person convicted of selling 28 grams of cocaine automatically received a minimum sentence of five years in prison. A judge could not be flexible for a first-time offender or for any other reason. Many of these new mandatory minimum sentencing guidelines were directed at drug-related crime.

Over time, as more and more people received these mandatory minimum sentences, the US prison population skyrocketed. As a result of this increase, taxpayers today spend $80 billion dollars each year on correctional facilities ranging from local jails to federal penitentiaries.[5] A 2016 report predicted that at some point in their lives, more than five million American children would have at least one parent in prison.[6] These statistics have led many people to strongly advocate for prison reform. Activists aim to make the criminal justice system fairer and to improve living conditions in prisons.

In 2018, US jails and prisons held almost 2.3 million people.[8] Cities and counties operated 3,163 local jails in the United States. These facilities held 731,000 inmates in 2018.[9] State and federal governments manage most prisons. State prisons hold criminals who have broken state laws. The United States has 1,719 state prisons. The majority of convicted criminals—1.3 million people—serve their

Some people who advocate for prison reform suggest alternatives to incarceration, in efforts to reduce the United States' prison population.

sentences in state prisons.[10] When people are convicted of breaking federal laws, they go to federal prison. The United States has 122 federal prisons.[11] Approximately 225,000 convicted criminals are incarcerated in federal prisons.[12]

SECURITY LEVELS

Prison security levels directly affect how inmates live. Prisons have a variety of security levels, and an inmate's criminal history determines his or her placement. Minimum-security prisons, also known as prison camps, are for nonviolent offenders. These inmates live in dormitories rather than prison cells. The ratio of guards to inmates is low. Inmates have a high level of freedom to move around the facility. Most inmates have fewer than ten years left on their sentences.[13]

The most common type of prison is low security, which is a step above minimum security. Low-security prisons are often called correctional institutions.

JAILS VS. PRISONS

The terms *jail* and *prison* are sometimes used interchangeably. But they are not the same. Jails mostly house people moving through the criminal justice system, such as people awaiting trial. Sometimes people serve their sentences in a jail. This might happen when a person has a short sentence, such as for a misdemeanor crime. Most people stay in jail for a short time, as opposed to prison, where people are usually incarcerated for longer periods of time. Most people in prison are not waiting for trial; they have been convicted. Usually prison inmates are serving long sentences for felonies.

More than one-third of prisoners in the United States were held in low-security facilities as of 2018.[14] Life there is similar to life at minimum-security facilities. The main difference is a higher ratio of guards to inmates. This is because inmates in low-security prisons may have a history of violence, which could include convictions for crimes such as assault or murder. Additionally, there is at least one row of security fencing surrounding these facilities. Most offenders in low-security prisons have fewer than 20 years left on their sentences.[15]

Like low-security prisons, medium-security prisons are often referred to as correctional institutions. Many of their inmates have a long history of crime and violence. This requires a high ratio of guards to inmates. Electronic alarms, armed patrols, and fences topped with razor wire guard medium-security facilities. Inmates live in locked cells and are only free to leave their cells during specific times of the day. Inmates in these facilities usually have at least 30 years left on their sentences.[16]

SECURITY SCORES

Convicts are placed in prisons based on a formula that takes into account their crime, age, arrest history, and violence level. The higher the score, the more security a prisoner requires. For example, a prisoner with a history of escape attempts would get five points added to the score.

High-security prisons, also known as penitentiaries, house the most dangerous and violent criminals. These facilities have a tight level of security. A sturdy wall with guard towers or multiple rows of reinforced fences secure the prison's perimeter. These facilities have the highest ratio of guards to inmates, and these inmates spend most of their time in their cells. When the inmates are allowed to leave their cells, guards closely monitor their movements.

At the highest end of the security spectrum is a supermax prison. The US Penitentiary Administrative Maximum Facility (ADX) in Florence, Colorado, is the nation's only federal supermax prison. It opened in 1994 and houses

The Federal Correctional Institution in Danbury, Connecticut, is a low-security prison.

the criminals who are considered to be the most dangerous in the nation. Life for the more than 400 inmates inside the ADX is different than daily life in other prisons. Inmates spend up to 23 hours of the day alone in their cells. Meals, exercise, and all other activities are done in solitary confinement. "The Supermax is life after death," said Robert Hood, who served as the ADX warden from 2002 to 2005. "It's long term. . . . In my opinion, it's far much worse than death."[17]

No matter where a prisoner is incarcerated, daily life in prison is an adjustment. Prisoners live by rigid schedules that tell them when to eat, work, and sleep. Privacy is scarce, and racism and violence are rampant. To survive, many prisoners must learn an entirely new way of life.

DISCUSSION STARTERS

- How can firsthand perspectives about prison life—such as *Ear Hustle*—change the way people think about prisoners? Why?
- How are mandatory sentencing guidelines and mass incarceration connected? Would changing the guidelines reduce the prison population? Why or why not?
- When people enter prison, their daily life changes dramatically. What do you think would be the hardest change to get used to?

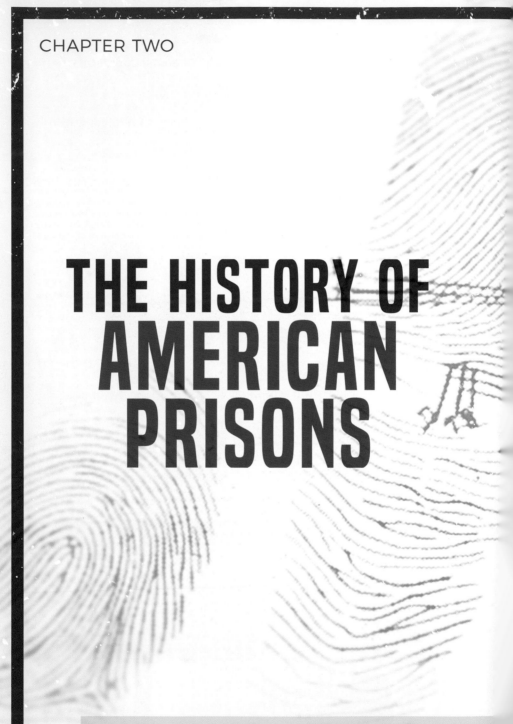

CHAPTER TWO

THE HISTORY OF AMERICAN PRISONS

San Quentin prison inmates listen to the radio in their cell in 1941.

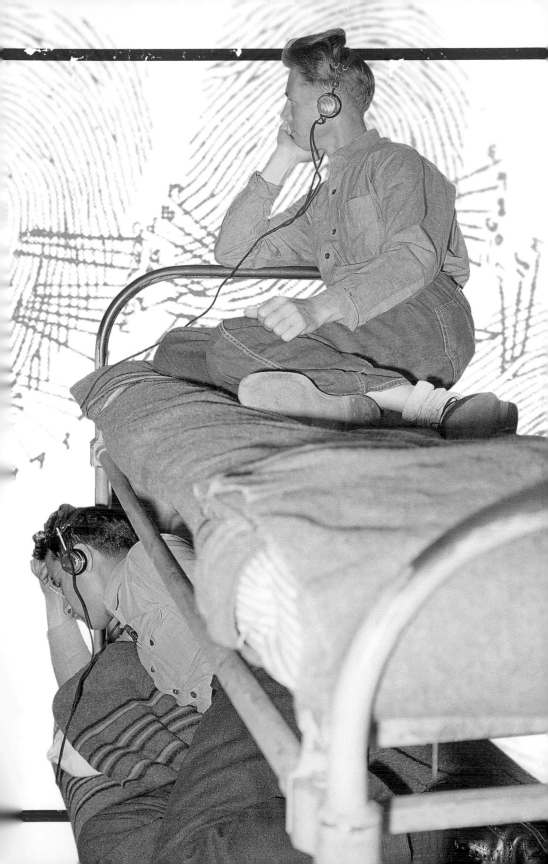

The world's first modern prison—Eastern State Penitentiary in Pennsylvania—did not open until 1829. Jails existed before this time, but they played a limited role. Jails held accused criminals until a trial could take place. Sometimes people also spent time in jail if they owed large debts. But locking up a criminal in a jail cell was a rare punishment.

In colonial America, most criminals served their sentences in public. A common sentence was time in the stocks. Stocks were wooden structures that confined a

Pillories were a common form of punishment for criminals in colonial America.

criminal's feet. Similarly, pillories confined criminals by their wrists and necks. Stocks and pillories usually stood in public areas, such as a town square. Citizens could walk by and stare, spit, or jeer at the person who was being punished.

For more serious crimes or repeat offenders, judges often demanded corporal punishment. This commonly took the form of public whippings. Sometimes criminals had their ears cut off, and some had their nostrils slit. Some were branded on their cheeks or hands. A thief would receive a *T*, and someone who killed another person might receive an *M* for manslaughter.

Most of the people who received these harsh sentences were members of the lower social classes. Wealthy offenders often paid fines to avoid being publicly shamed or permanently disfigured. Public shame was the driving force behind these types of punishments.

NEW IDEAS

After the United States gained independence through the American Revolutionary

THE SCARLET LETTER

In 1850, American author Nathaniel Hawthorne wrote one of his most famous novels, *The Scarlet Letter*. The story's main character, Hester Prynne, had a child with another man while her husband was away. As a result, she was sentenced to wear a scarlet-colored letter *A* in public to mark her as an adulteress. This novel allows readers to reflect on the nation's early criminal justice system, its form of punishment, and the toll it took on its victims.

CRITICISM

Although many Americans embraced prisons as a solution to crime, not all people agreed. When English author Charles Dickens toured the United States in 1842, he visited Philadelphia's Eastern State Penitentiary. Dickens found the situation there dire, and he wrote about it in his work titled *American Notes*:

> The system here is rigid, strict, and hopeless solitary confinement. I believe it, in its effects, to be cruel and wrong. In its intention, I am well convinced that it is kind, humane, and meant for reformation; but I am persuaded that those who devised this system of prison discipline, and those benevolent gentlemen who carry it to execution, do not know what it is that they are doing. . . . It is my fixed opinion that those who have undergone this punishment, must pass into society again morally unhealthy and diseased.[1]

War (1775–1783), the criminal justice system began to change. Cities grew larger and more impersonal, which meant public shaming did not have the same effect that it once had. The use of corporal punishment also fell out of favor. Citizens started to view whipping and branding as barbaric. And in a country that had struggled hard for independence, taking away a criminal's freedom seemed like a more appropriate punishment than earlier methods.

Ideas of what caused people to commit crimes changed, too. Many colonists had believed that people committed crimes because they were morally weak or were tempted by evil. After the United States gained independence, many Americans grew to believe society itself caused crime. They argued that parents, churches, and schools had failed to properly train some citizens to lead moral, productive lives, and, as a result, these improperly trained people went on to commit crimes. Dorothea Dix, an outspoken social reformer of the time, said, "It is to the defects of our social organization, to the multiplied and multiplying temptations to crime that we chiefly owe the increase of evil doers."[2]

Beginning in the 1800s, reformers began to believe that if society had failed criminals, society could also rehabilitate them. Prison sentences became an opportunity to reshape criminals into upstanding citizens. To accomplish this, early prisons relied heavily on routines and military-style discipline. Prisoners often lived alone in their cells, like in modern solitary confinement. Visitors to early prisons commented that despite being among hundreds of prisoners, an eerie quiet permeated the prison.

The idea of reform and discipline—rather than public shame and corporal punishment—appealed to Americans.

EASTERN STATE PENITENTIARY

Eastern State Penitentiary (ESP) was built in response to the appalling conditions at the Walnut Street Jail in Philadelphia, Pennsylvania. At the jail, convicts were thrown into dirty, overcrowded cells. Rape, murder, and theft were common there.

ESP was different. It used solitude to encourage criminals to repent. Criminals lived alone in cells, and they could not talk to other inmates. ESP was clean, bright, and modern. The building itself was revolutionary. It had a central hub with seven cellblocks shooting out of it, like spokes on a wheel. Several prisons built after this point followed the ESP model.

The new nation was eager to try out a new criminal justice system. It was a massive experiment, but it would ultimately lead to the world's first modern prison system. Americans were optimistic that this new system of criminal justice would improve society. As a result, state lawmakers began to approve funds for the creation of dozens of prisons.

A MODERN SYSTEM

As the nation expanded, the prison system changed again. The American population more than doubled between 1880 and 1920. As American cities grew, so did crime rates. Prisons became crowded, and prisoners began to share cells. Although strict discipline remained, the focus was no longer on rehabilitation. Instead, prisons served to corral dangerous criminals in an effort to keep cities safe.

State governments had originally carried the burden of building and maintaining prisons and caring for the inmates. But as the country grew, the federal government played a larger role. New federal laws regarding taxes, immigration, and other issues affected more citizens. People found guilty of violating federal laws were sent to newly constructed federal prisons. In 1889, federal courts had heard 14,588 criminal cases.[3] That number more than tripled in 65 years, ballooning to 48,856 federal criminal cases by 1954.[4]

Today, the United States incarcerates its citizens at a higher rate than any other nation in the world. A 2018 report from the advocacy group Prison Policy Initiative showed that approximately 70 percent of all convicted criminals received prison time rather than other forms of restitution, such as fines or community service.[5] But not everyone is convinced that mass incarceration makes the nation safer. In his book *Locked In*, law professor John F. Pfaff states, "Mass incarceration is one of the biggest social problems the United States faces today; our sprawling prison system imposes staggering economic, social, political, and racial costs."[6]

DISCUSSION STARTERS

- Why were public shaming and corporal punishment effective consequences for breaking laws when the United States was a new nation? What changes in values led to the rise of prisons as punishment?
- Do you believe that criminals are a product of societal problems? Why or why not?
- Do you think giving offenders alternate forms of restitution rather than prison time is a good idea? Why or why not?

CHAPTER THREE

MASS INCARCERATION

An inmate is shackled at his wrists and legs as he's escorted by corrections officers through the Souza-Baranowski Correctional Center, a maximum-security prison in Shirley, Massachusetts.

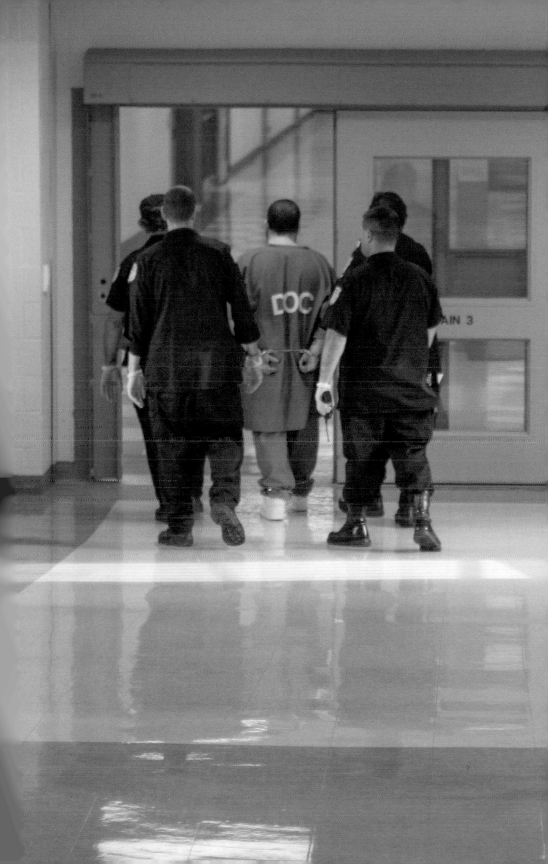

Over the past 40 years, the US criminal justice system has grown to heavily favor incarceration. More Americans are incarcerated now than at any other time in history. And the prison sentences they are serving are longer, too. The United States has created an extensive, multibillion-dollar prison system that facilitates mass incarceration. Lawyer and civil rights advocate Michelle Alexander explains:

> I think most Americans have no idea of the scale and scope of mass incarceration in the United States. Unless you're directly impacted by the system, unless you have a loved one who's behind bars, unless you've done time yourself, unless you have a family member who's been branded a criminal and felon and can't get work, can't find housing, [is] denied even food stamps to survive, unless the system directly touches you, it's hard to even imagine that something of this scope and scale could even exist.[1]

Mass incarceration did not happen overnight. It took decades of changes in policies and laws to set it into motion. Between the 1960s and 1980s, the United States as a whole experienced a spike in crime rates. This was partly because of changing criminal justice policies, such as harsher laws against drugs. Citizens demanded a change, and politicians

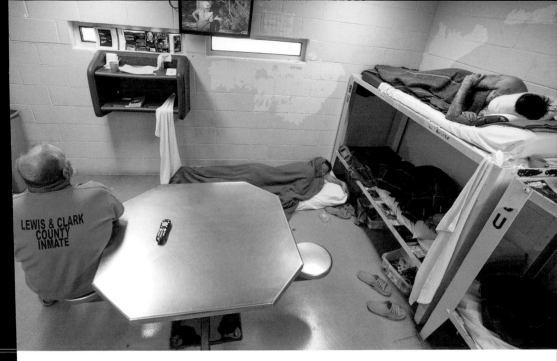

Mass incarceration has led to overcrowding in many US prisons and jails.

and law enforcement began a decades-long crusade against crime. The result was mass incarceration, seen in a nationwide prison population that quadrupled between 1980 and 2013.[2]

THE WAR ON DRUGS

The first stirrings of a change in the criminal justice system began in the 1960s. It was a decade of unrest in the United States. The civil rights movement, which sought equal treatment for people of all races, polarized the nation. Tensions between black and white citizens ran high. People across the country were also angry about the United States' involvement in the Vietnam War (1954–1975). All of this discontent led to riots, political protests, and street violence. Crimes such as robberies and murders increased during this time period.

By the time Americans voted for president in November 1968, law and order had become one of the most important issues in the nation. Richard Nixon narrowly won the election, running on a platform that promised to get tough on crime. As part of this effort, Nixon declared a War on Drugs in June 1971. It increased federal resources for drug agencies, and it also created mandatory minimum sentences for drug-related offenses. This kicked off what would become a pattern of mass incarceration.

The Nixon administration framed its programs as a fight against crime. But an interview that appeared in a 2016

Former president Richard Nixon initiated the US government's War on Drugs in 1971.

Harper's Magazine article revealed different motivations. Dan Baum, the article's writer, had interviewed John Ehrlichman, a former Nixon aide, back in 1994. Ehrlichman spoke about the drug policies of the time, saying, "The Nixon campaign in 1968, and the Nixon White House after that, had two enemies: the antiwar left and black people. . . . We knew we couldn't make it illegal to be either against the war or black, but by getting the public to associate the hippies with marijuana and blacks with heroin, and then criminalizing both heavily, we could disrupt those communities."[4] That effort to disrupt African American communities worked, considering the fact that black people are still disproportionately incarcerated today.

VIEWS CHANGE BUT HARSH LAWS REMAIN

Still, through the 1970s, the antidrug movement surged forward. Under President Ronald Reagan, federal funding for the criminal justice system increased. In 1985, for example, the criminal justice budget increased by $200 million. It allowed the Drug Enforcement Agency (DEA) and the Federal Bureau of Investigation (FBI) to hire hundreds of new agents. The increase also helped fund the construction of new prisons.

A warden shows media reporters inside a Tennessee prison in 1977.

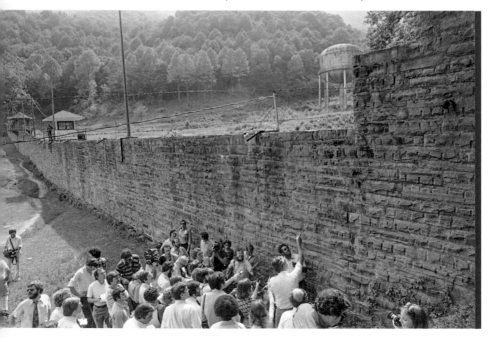

During this time, new sentencing laws also took effect. These harsh, punitive laws demanded mandatory minimum sentences for drug offenses, which then led to more people being arrested and kept imprisoned for longer periods of time. Between 1980 and 1997, the number of people imprisoned for nonviolent drug offenses rose from 50,000 to 400,000.[5] In 1986, a federal drug crimes offender spent an average of 22 months in prison. By 2004, that figure had increased to 62 months.[6]

In the following years, society's views on how to handle drug-related crimes gradually shifted. Many health-care experts started to promote rehabilitation rather than incarceration for people involved with drugs, such as those convicted of low-level drug offenses. But the harsh laws remained in place. Politicians had said mandatory minimum sentences were created to imprison high-level drug traffickers and dealers. However, more than one-half of the people incarcerated for drug crimes

TYPES OF CRIMES

In federal prisons, people convicted of drug crimes make up the largest percentage of offenders. Trafficking, manufacturing, and distributing drugs are the most common crimes that land people in federal prison. State prison populations are different. The largest percentage of offenders in state prisons includes people who have been convicted of violent crimes. These include crimes such as manslaughter, rape, and aggravated assault.[7]

PRISON COSTS

California has the most expensive state prison system in the country. In 2017, it cost $75,560 per year to house one inmate in a California prison. To put that in perspective, a student could attend Harvard University for one year—including tuition, room and board, and other campus expenses—for $2,000 less than this.[11] In an effort to reduce prison spending, California and many other states are looking at ways to reform prisons. Some of these reforms include releasing more low-level, nonviolent offenders on parole.

were convicted on low-level, nonviolent offenses. As the laws have been slow to change, incarceration rates remain high.

As convictions increased and sentences grew in the 1980s and 1990s, states needed to figure out where to put all the new inmates. In a July 2015 Instagram post that advocated for prison reform, Senator Cory Booker of New Jersey commented on how fast the system grew. "We built a new prison every 10 days between 1990 and 2005 to keep up with our mass incarceration explosion of nonviolent offenders," he said, referring to the 544 state and federal prisons built during that time period.[8]

Building all those new prisons was expensive, and the cost fell on taxpayers. In addition to construction costs, taxpayers continue to pay for housing each inmate. In 2015, the average cost to house one prisoner in the United States was $33,274.[9] By comparison, in 2015 Americans earned an average yearly income of $30,622.[10] It cost nearly as much to employ a person as to incarcerate him. The majority of the money that goes to prisons—68 percent—pays for the salaries and benefits for prison guards and staff.[12] The remaining money pays for building maintenance, health care, and other prison services.

Mass incarceration has affected far more than taxpayers' wallets. It has had a profound effect on criminal offenders' families, particularly their children. As of January 2017, approximately 2.7 million children living in the United States had a parent in prison.[13] Research shows that these children are at a high risk for dropping out of school and going to jail themselves. It is a cycle that is hard to break.

DISCUSSION STARTERS

- How did the Vietnam War and the civil rights movement influence laws that led to mass incarceration?
- What role do drugs play in mass incarceration? Would legalizing drugs such as marijuana reduce prison rates?
- Mass incarceration has a ripple effect. What are some of its effects on taxpayers, communities, and families?

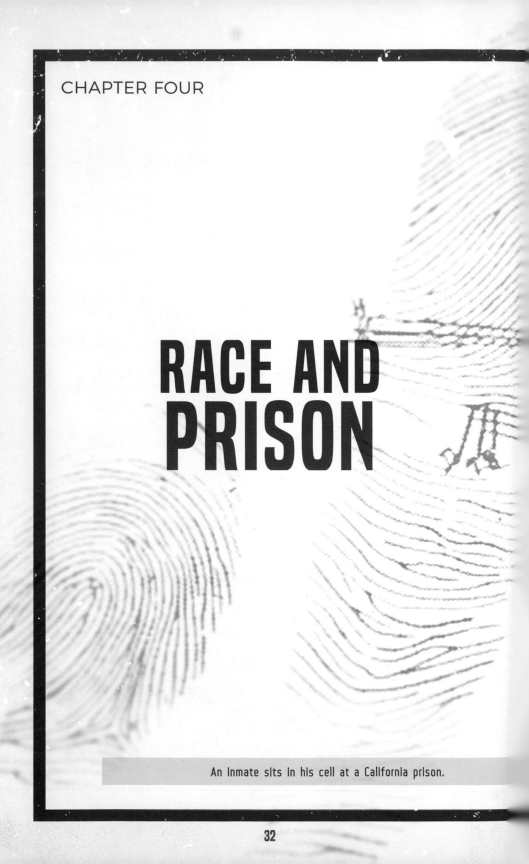

CHAPTER FOUR

RACE AND PRISON

An inmate sits in his cell at a California prison.

C ritics of mass incarceration hope to change many aspects of the US prison system—high costs, rising levels of inmate violence, and a cycle of repeat offenders. Perhaps one of the biggest problems, however, is that mass incarceration disproportionately affects people of color, especially African Americans. The harsh sentencing laws of the past 40 years have affected black people more than people of any other race. People of color are more likely to be arrested than white people. And, once arrested, they are more likely to be convicted and receive longer prison sentences.

In the United States, a black person is five times more likely to be incarcerated than a white person. Although black people make up only 13 percent of the US population, they represent 40 percent of inmates.[1] "The reality is that today there are more African Americans under correctional control in prison or jail, on probation or parole, than

AVA DUVERNAY'S *13TH*

Ava DuVernay's 2016 documentary *13th* reveals deep-rooted institutional racism against black people within the criminal justice system. The award-winning film suggests mass incarceration is a form of modern slavery. "When you take apart some of the pieces of what slavery was, you see they are mirroring the current day. We are re-enslaved by the millions," DuVernay, who is black, told the *New York Times*. "We are turning our eyes away from the horrors of what's happening inside. We are participating as slave masters because we consume products and elect politicians and are complicit in enabling the system. So it's not a one-to-one comparison, it's an emotional comparison."[2]

were enslaved in 1850, a decade before the Civil War began,"

says lawyer and civil rights advocate Michelle Alexander.[3]

THE EFFECT OF POVERTY

The reasons behind this problem are complex. But, many

experts believe urban poverty, or concentrated poverty in

city neighborhoods, is a major factor. In the United States,

urban poverty affects the African American community

more than any other. Approximately two-thirds of African

American children born between 1985 and 2000 grew up

in neighborhoods with at least 20 percent of residents

In American cities, poverty affects people of color at a higher rate than
white people.

BLACK LIVES MATTER

Three black activists—Alicia Garza, Patrisse Cullors, and Opal Tometi—started a social movement in 2013 called Black Lives Matter. They created it in response to the acquittal of George Zimmerman, a neighborhood watch captain who shot and killed an unarmed black 17-year-old, Trayvon Martin.

Anger over Zimmerman's acquittal drew attention to the inequalities that black people face in the criminal justice system. For example, in 2016, African Americans were incarcerated at five times the rate of white people. In five states—Iowa, Minnesota, New Jersey, Vermont, and Wisconsin—that rate jumps to 10 times. Experts believe that these disparities are partly due to racial bias in policing. These problems are what many Americans want to fight today by joining groups such as Black Lives Matter. As of 2018, Black Lives Matter had more than 40 local chapters across the United States.[6]

living in poverty. In comparison, white children born in those same years had only a 6 percent chance of living in a neighborhood with similar poverty levels.[4]

A 2014 Prison Policy Initiative study looked at the average income of people before they were incarcerated. The study then compared that data to the average incomes of people who were not in prison. The gap in earnings was significant. Incarcerated men of all races had earned an average yearly salary of $19,650. In contrast, their nonincarcerated peers had earned $41,250.[5] This shows that people who end up in prison make less money on average than people who are not incarcerated.

This link between poverty and prison is complicated, and there are many aspects of poverty that contribute to the likelihood of incarceration. People living in urban poverty often have less access to good-quality public education and high-paying jobs. Violence, crime, drugs, and gangs are more common in areas of high urban poverty. And policing levels are often much higher in these areas than in suburban and rural areas, which makes it more likely for people to be arrested. Under all of these circumstances, the high likelihood of incarceration becomes a cycle that's hard to break.

"In these communities, where incarceration has become so normalized, the system operates practically from cradle to

Michelle Alexander, lawyer and civil rights activist

grave," Alexander says. "When you're born, your parent has likely already spent time behind bars. . . . And that's where it begins. It sends this message that whether you follow the rules or you don't, you're going to jail—just like your uncle, just like your father, just like your brother, just like your neighbor. You, too, are going to jail. It's part of your destiny."[7]

POLICING

However, poverty is not the only factor. Policing also plays a role. In the early 1990s, an idea known as the broken windows theory gained popularity in policing. It is based on the work of Stanford University psychologist Philip Zimbardo. In 1969, he conducted an experiment in which he left two identical cars parked on the street. One was in a poor neighborhood in New York. The other was in a wealthy neighborhood in California.

The car in New York sat for ten minutes before people began attacking it. They smashed the windows and stripped it for parts. Meanwhile, the car in California remained untouched for a week. Next, Zimbardo smashed the windows of the California car with a sledgehammer. Within minutes, people stripped the California car just as quickly as

The broken windows theory is the idea that small signs of disorder, such as broken car windows, can cause people to feel more comfortable engaging in higher levels of disorder or crime.

they had done to the one in New York. The only difference

was the broken windows.

Criminologists George Kelling and James Wilson

wondered whether the results of this experiment could be

applied to policing. "The idea [is] that once disorder begins,

it doesn't matter what the neighborhood is, things can begin

to get out of control," Kelling said.[8] Broken windows, graffiti,

and loitering are all signs of disorder. Kelling and Wilson

theorized that if police put a stop to these relatively small

issues, maybe larger crimes would stop, too.

This led to a law enforcement approach known as "broken windows policing," which directs police to focus on small but visible criminal activity. Police are encouraged to arrest or fine people committing graffiti and vandalism. The idea is that the public will see these arrests and be reminded of police presence. Then, people will be less likely to commit larger and more serious crimes.

New York City was one of the first places to put this idea into practice. City police began arresting more people for misdemeanors, and violent crimes decreased. Based on this success, police started practicing an offshoot of the broken windows theory called "stop and frisk." Police officers could stop and frisk anyone they deemed suspicious—even if the person was not committing a crime. These ideas may have sounded good in theory. But in practice, they revealed deep racial bias.

In New York City, African Americans and Hispanic people made up 85 percent of all stop and frisk encounters.[9] Police

STOP AND FRISK RULED UNCONSTITUTIONAL

At its height in 2011, New York City police officers stopped residents 684,000 times as part of their stop and frisk policy.[10] Outrage against the policy led to a lawsuit in a federal district court in Manhattan. The court ruled that the way officers had carried out the stop and frisk policy between 2005 and 2013 had been unconstitutional and racially discriminatory. Officers had stopped people based solely on their race, rather than on suspicion of criminal wrongdoing.

officers, whether they were consciously aware of it or not, made the choice to stop more black and Latino people under the stop and frisk policy. The encounters often resulted in arrests, which contributed to a disproportionate number of black and Latino people being incarcerated. In communities where stop and frisk was common, people lived in fear of being stopped. "They done mess your whole life up and this is what they do," said one New York resident about policing policies. "They arrest you and build up all these

Many people including the Rev. Al Sharpton, *center*, protested against the New York City Police Department's stop and frisk policy.

little, petty things . . . and after a certain time, now okay, you have three of these, it's a felony. When you put a felony on somebody you're telling a person basically you're just a hard-core criminal."[11]

PRISON CULTURE AND RACE

The influence of race in the criminal justice system extends beyond arrest and conviction rates. In prison, race is one of the most dominating factors in how inmates socialize. In most cases, it is the prisoners themselves who instigate the segregation. The prison yard, dining tables, and even showers tend to be divided along racial lines. And if violence or disrespect occurs among inmates, racial groups generally stand up for each other. Jerry Metcalf, a Michigan man serving time for second-degree murder, explained to journalist Eli Hager:

> *Everything in here is about race—and I mean everything. Whites have their side of the chow hall, blacks have their side of the chow hall. Whites use the white barber, blacks use the black barber. It's the 1950s in here—I mean, we share drinking fountains, but not much else. . . . The only difference between prison in 2017 and a segregated 1950s is the fact that whites are often the minorities behind bars.[12]*

For many years in California prisons, guards placed inmates in cell blocks based on their races. They did this as a way to reduce violence and maintain order among the different racial groups, and it was fairly successful. In 2005, the US Supreme Court ordered California officials to stop segregating inmates based on race. For many of the inmates who had been in prison for decades, the change was hard to adjust to.

THE CHINO PRISON RIOT

Amid the desegregation of California prisons, officials faced a flurry of interracial violence between inmates. One of the most extreme examples happened in 2009 at a prison in Chino, California. That August, a Latino gang and an African American gang engaged in a fight that resulted in the destruction of two buildings, including a dormitory that was burned down. There were 240 inmates injured in the fight.[13]

DISCUSSION STARTERS

- What role does race play in the criminal justice system? What are some possible solutions to ensure people of all races are treated equally?

- What is the link between urban poverty and crime? Would reducing urban poverty reduce crime rates, too?

- Prisons are often sharply divided by racial lines, but most of the racial divisions are created and upheld by the prisoners themselves. Why do you think this happens?

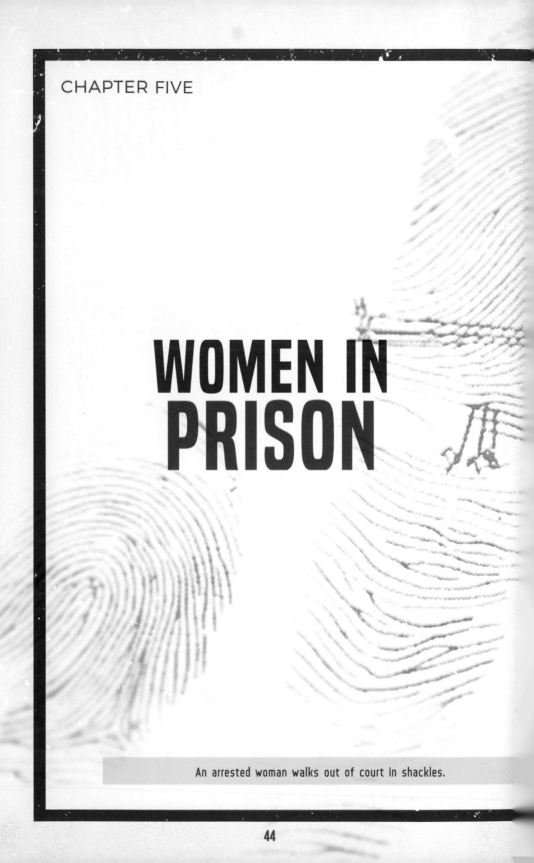

CHAPTER FIVE

WOMEN IN PRISON

An arrested woman walks out of court in shackles.

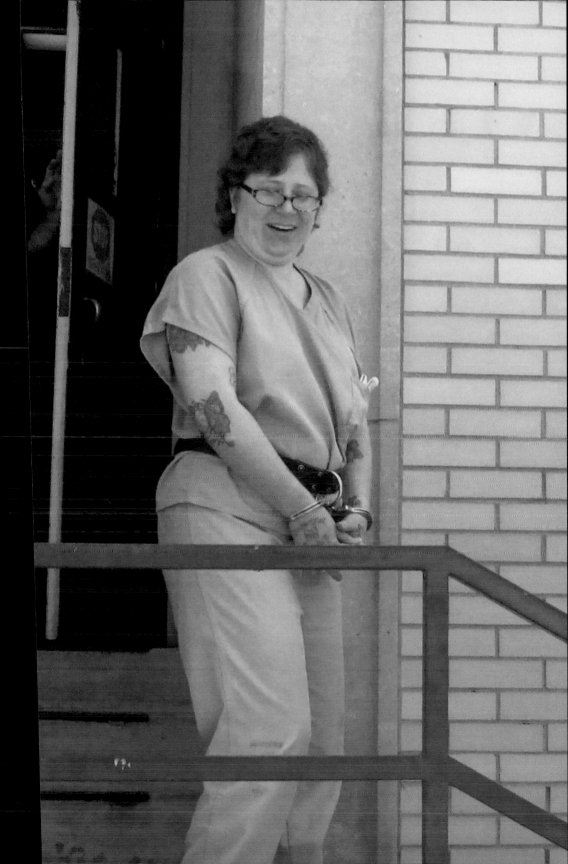

W omen make up a small portion of convicted offenders in the United States. However, they are not immune from the wave of mass incarceration that has surged across the country. Today, women are the fastest-growing segment of the prison population. Between 1978 and 2015, the number of women behind bars increased by 834 percent. That is more than double the growth of incarceration rates of men for the same period.[1] The majority of female inmates are nonviolent, first-time offenders.

The Nacogdoches County Jail in Texas was originally designed to house men, but part of the facility was changed to house women as a result of more women being arrested.

Women's prisons are separate from men's prisons, so facilities and programs vary.

Because men make up the majority of inmates, prison systems and programs are designed with them in mind. Women behind bars often find themselves in a system that does not fully understand the challenges they face. Female inmates have higher rates of mental illnesses, disease, past abuse, and substance abuse problems than their male counterparts. Many women do not get the help they need to overcome these problems. Less than one-half of women in prison with a history of substance abuse receive treatment. And less than one-quarter of women with psychiatric problems receive adequate mental health care while incarcerated.[2] Because the prison system struggles to treat these problems, many women find themselves worse off than before they entered.

Elizabeth Swavola, author of the 2016 report *Overlooked: Women and Jails in the Age of Reform*, explained the situation:

FEMALE INMATES AND RACE

As with male inmates, a high percentage of incarcerated women are people of color. Across the nation, two-thirds of female inmates are women of color. Of that group, black women make up 44 percent, Hispanic women are 15 percent, and women of other racial or ethnic backgrounds are 5 percent.[3] Most of those women are in their 30s with at least one child.[4] White women make up the remaining 36 percent of female prisoners.

"Jails are designed for men, because they're the majority of who is there. But that makes it very difficult on women. [Women] are coming with a whole host of disadvantages, and many of those disadvantages led to their criminal justice involvement, and then are deepened by the criminal justice system itself."[5]

MOTHERHOOD

One of the biggest challenges for incarcerated women is being a parent. Nearly 80 percent of all incarcerated women are mothers.[6] Most of them are single parents who are the full-time caregivers for their children.[7] When these women enter prison, their children face an uncertain future. Some live with family members, while others live in foster homes. These children's lives are often unstable.

Loretta Lynch, who was attorney general under President Barack Obama, discussed this growing concern in a 2016 speech at the White House regarding women and the criminal justice system. "Put simply, we know that when we incarcerate a woman we often are truly incarcerating a family, in terms of the far-reaching effect on her children, her community, and her entire family network," Lynch said.[8]

Former attorney general Loretta Lynch spoke out about the need for the US prison system to better serve incarcerated women.

Lavette Mayes, an Illinois woman, was one of those mothers. In 2015, the single mother of two was arrested on an aggravated battery charge in connection with a fight that occurred while she was going through a divorce. After being booked into a Chicago jail, she had the option of paying 10 percent of her bail, which amounted to $25,000, in order to be released. But she couldn't afford it. As a result, she remained incarcerated. She spent more than a year in jail until an organization called the Chicago Community Bond Fund stepped in to help. In 2016, the organization gave Mayes a grant to cover her bail costs. Though she was finally able to return to her children, she struggled to make their lives feel normal again. Her children worried that when she left the house, she would not return.

"It tears your family apart," said Mayes, reflecting on her time behind bars. "And when you get out, it tears your family apart again. . . . It took two years out of my life, out of my family, out of my community. It was like

WHAT IS BAIL?

When police officers arrest someone, they bring the person to jail. If the inmate wants to be released while awaiting trial, a judge may allow him or her to post bail. Judges set the dollar amount of an inmate's bail. Bail amounts are generally higher for more serious crimes. When inmates are released on bail, they promise to attend their court dates. If they appear at the required court dates, their money is returned after their cases are resolved. If they fail to appear in court, they forfeit the bail money.

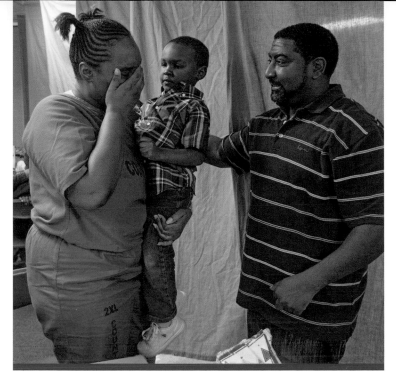

An inmate cries as her son and brother visit her during a supervised event at the Harris County Sheriff's Office in Houston, Texas, in 2011.

birthing them again. I had never been away from them for that amount of time."[9]

Mayes is not alone in the struggle to make bail. Nearly 60 percent of women in jail are awaiting trial. They have not yet been convicted of any crimes. The reason this number is so high has little to do with the type of crimes the women committed. It has much more to do with lacking the money to pay for bail. A typical cost of bail is approximately $10,000. A 2016 study showed that women who found themselves in jail and unable to afford bail earned a median income of $11,071 yearly.[10] For these women, trying to come up with nearly an entire year's wages on short notice is practically impossible. As a result, these women have no option but to stay in jail. And when women have to stay in jail, it disrupts their families and may lead to job loss.

PROBATION AND JAIL

Once convicted, women are more likely than men to be sentenced to probation rather than jail time. Probation allows women to care for their children and keep their jobs. However, they must check in with a probation officer regularly, and they must follow the terms of their probation. Terms of probation often require offenders to stay off drugs, avoid criminal activity, and to attend rehabilitation classes. If they violate these terms, they are incarcerated.

Probation also comes with high financial costs. Probation involves a number of fees, like bail, which many women cannot afford to pay. These fees vary, but they can range from a few hundred dollars to several thousand. Failing to pay the fees is a violation of the probation terms. It can result in the woman being rearrested and jailed. Many women on probation also struggle to afford childcare while they meet with their probation officers. If the women cannot keep their appointments for this reason, they are violating their probation terms.

These financial costs can disproportionately affect women of color. This is a result of ongoing racial discrimination, particularly toward impoverished women. Writer Rachel Costa explains, "Since incarceration commonly occurs in lower levels of society, the families with the fewest means are the ones forced to cope with such a difficult situation."[11]

Despite the high probation rate, approximately 219,000 women were incarcerated in 2017. Whereas men are more likely to be incarcerated in state prisons, women are fairly evenly divided between state jails and prisons. More than one-half of the women in jails are awaiting trial. Approximately one-quarter of women who are convicted serve out their sentences in jails. In contrast, when looking at all convicts, only 10 percent go to jails rather than prisons.[12]

DIFFERENT NEEDS

One challenge unique to female prisoners is their need for menstrual hygiene products. Female prisoners in many states do not have access to enough menstrual hygiene supplies. For example, as of 2017, women in Arizona state prisons received only 12 pads per month. If they wanted more, they had to buy them at their prison. Purchasing a box of 16 pads cost approximately 21 hours' worth of wages.

State prisons are slowly starting to change this by offering free menstrual supplies. "Menstrual hygiene products should not be considered a luxury," said Maryland senator Susan Lee, who fought for changes. She urged fellow lawmakers to "do more to prevent dehumanizing situations where women inmates don't have sanitary necessities."[13]

PREGNANCY AND PRISON

Incarcerated women have many health-care needs that differ from those of men, and prisons are often not equipped to handle these women's needs. This is particularly true for pregnant women. Each year approximately 9,000 pregnant women are incarcerated.[14] But few prisons offer programs for pregnant women. After a baby is born, he or she may be placed with a family member or in a foster home.

The children born to incarcerated women face unique challenges. Most women's prisons are located in rural areas, far from the prisoners' homes. Transportation for visits can be expensive and hard to plan, and some caregivers may not be able to take time off from work to bring a baby to visit his or her mother in prison. As a result, only one-half of all mothers in prison receive visits from their children. This makes it difficult for mothers to maintain healthy bonds with their children. And for the children, this can cause psychological problems, drug use, and even criminal activity that results in incarceration later in life.

Recently, lawmakers have been working to solve these problems. One solution has come in the form of eight Moms and Babies prison programs across the country.

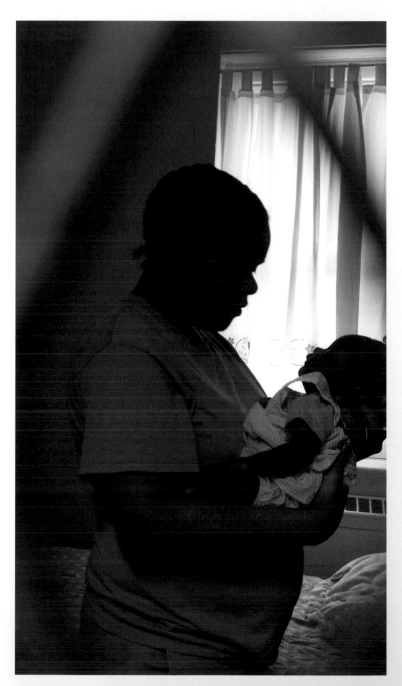

An inmate at the Indiana Women's Prison holds her baby in her prison cell.

These programs, which are being conducted on a trial basis, are designed for women who have given birth while incarcerated. To qualify, the women must have committed nonviolent crimes and have sentences less than two years in length.

The goal of this program is to support the bond between mothers and babies, bring peace to families, and reduce recidivism. The program works by allowing babies to live in prison with their mothers. Women in the program still live in prison cells, but the cells are outfitted with cribs and other baby gear. The prison provides childcare while the women take classes. The program also allows participants to be with other new moms and learn parenting skills.

One prison trying the Moms and Babies program is the Decatur Correctional Center in Illinois. So far, the facility has seen positive results. More than 90 women have completed the program. Only two of them have been reincarcerated within three

DESTINY DOUD

Destiny Doud participated in the Moms and Babies program at Decatur Correctional Center in Illinois. In October 2016, Doud was arrested for trafficking methamphetamine across state lines. Shortly after her conviction, the 21-year-old learned she was pregnant. After giving birth, Doud thought she would have only 48 hours to spend with her daughter. Just as she was about to turn her daughter over to relatives, she learned that she qualified for the program. She has been grateful for the opportunity to be with her daughter and is hopeful for the future. "She reminds me that I have something that's great now," Doud said. "Something to live for."[15]

years after release. Programs at other facilities show similar results, with recidivism rates as low as 4 percent. "We have found that if there is going to be anything that keeps women from reoffending, it's going to be their bonds with their children," said Shelith Hansbro, the warden at the Decatur facility. "If we expect them to be successful, we need . . . to give them those tools they need to be successful."[16]

DISCUSSION STARTERS

- Women are the fastest-growing segment of the prison population. What kinds of challenges do they face in prison that are different from those faced by male prisoners?

- Why do you think poverty contributes to the rising rates of female prisoners?

- Probation makes it easier for women convicted of crimes to continue caring for their children and working. But mothers on probation still face real challenges. Is there a way to improve the difficulties mothers on probation face? If so, in what ways might this be done?

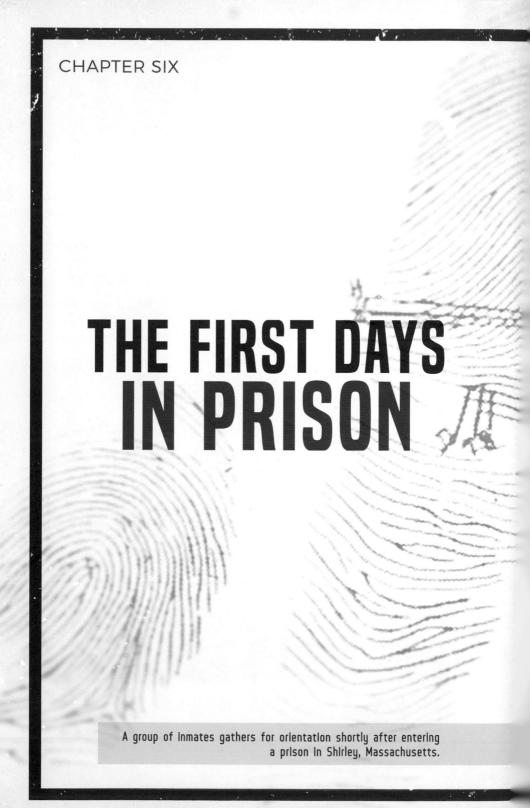

CHAPTER SIX

THE FIRST DAYS IN PRISON

A group of inmates gathers for orientation shortly after entering a prison in Shirley, Massachusetts.

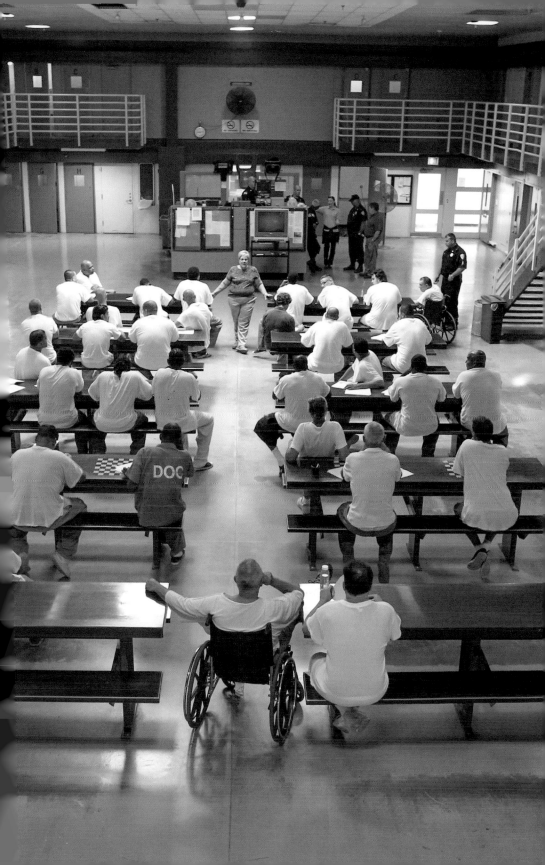

Though there are differences between the state and federal prison systems, the basic structure is similar. A convicted offender first makes his way through intake, which is the process of entering the prison system. The way a convicted offender arrives at prison depends on a number of factors. But the most important factor is whether the offender is considered dangerous to the community. For example, an offender convicted of aggravated assault is more likely to be considered dangerous than someone convicted of fraud or counterfeiting.

Dozens of new inmates stand together after arriving at the Georgia Diagnostic and Classification Prison in Jackson, Georgia.

If the offender poses no threat, a judge may allow him to go home for a few days after sentencing. This allows him to make final arrangements, such as getting finances in order or visiting with family, before going to prison. The offender will receive an official date and time to report to prison. He is responsible for getting himself there. This type of prison intake is called a self-surrender.

The path is different for convicted offenders who are at risk of running away or who may be dangerous. In those cases, the convicted offender remains in custody after sentencing, usually at a jail, until the date he is due in prison. Law enforcement officers or prison guards transport prisoners to the facility where they've been assigned. Sometimes the prisoners are transported by for-profit companies.

PRISON TRANSPORT VEHICLES

Sometimes law enforcement officers need to transport prisoners. This may happen when an inmate is transferred to a different facility, when a prisoner has to appear in court, or when a prisoner has an appointment at a special medical facility. In these situations, officers use prison transport vehicles (PTVs).

PTVs are specially designed cars, vans, and buses. A cage separates the driver from the passengers. Door handles and window controls are removed. The only way doors can be locked or unlocked is from the front of the vehicle. Depending on the situation, prisoners may wear extra restraints, such as handcuffs or leg irons, when in PTVs. This is a precaution against a prisoner who might try to escape or injure another passenger or a guard.

RECEIVING AND DISCHARGE UNIT

Once an inmate arrives at prison, he goes to the Receiving and Discharge Unit (R&D). There, he must disclose all the possessions he has with him. When entering prison, an inmate is allowed a limited number of items. These typically include medication, eyeglasses, wedding bands without stones, and legal documents. Anything else is considered contraband. Guards either throw it away or mail it to the prisoner's family. During R&D, an inmate also undergoes a body search. This is to make sure the prisoner has no contraband hidden in his body.

ADMISSION AND ORIENTATION PROGRAM

All prisons have formal rules and policies that everyone must follow closely to maintain order and safety. To learn these rules, all new inmates are put on Admission and Orientation (A&O) status for their first few weeks in prison. During this time, new prisoners go to meetings to learn about how the prison runs, what the rules are, and what programs are available. Inmates on A&O status also receive a handbook. It covers everything from daily schedules to the consequences for breaking a rule.

At this point, the prisoner receives supplies. The prison issues each inmate clothing, which includes socks, underwear, T-shirts, button-down shirts, pants, a winter jacket, and work boots. The color of the clothing depends on the prison. In addition, prisoners also receive a bedroll, sheets, towels, washcloths, and toiletries.

Inmates must be escorted by corrections officers as they enter or leave prison.

In prison slang, these supplies are referred to as a *fish kit* because new prisoners are known among other inmates as *fish*.

The first day also includes other administrative details. The prisoner is photographed and fingerprinted. Then he receives an identification card and prison number to use while he is an inmate. The prisoner also meets with prison officials. They inquire about any specific needs the prisoner has, such as a need for special medical care. Once all of these items have been taken care of, officials determine where within the prison the inmate will live.

LIVING QUARTERS

Living quarters differ slightly from prison to prison. However, each prison typically has small cells that each house two inmates. Within that confined space, a cell usually has a bunk, a desk bolted to the wall, a storage locker, and a metal toilet and sink. Some have small windows, too. The cells are organized into groups called blocks. Large prisons may have multiple blocks, each containing hundreds of cells. Smaller

An inmate shows his cell in the military veterans-only unit at the Jefferson County Detention Facility in Colorado.

prisons may have only a few blocks with dozens of cells each.

For people on the outside, it's hard to imagine just how small cells really are. On one episode of his podcast *Ear Hustle*, Earlonne Woods described his cell at San Quentin State Prison. "How big is a cell? It is like 4 feet by 9 feet. If I got my back on one wall, I can touch the other one. . . . I'll put it like this: you [and your cellmate] can't walk by each other. One person's got to sit on his bunk and the other person can walk by. It's like a little public storage."[1]

Inmates are responsible for keeping their cells clean and tidy. Prisons have strict requirements about how to do this. In federal prisons, beds must be made by 7:30 a.m. on weekdays and 10:00 a.m. on weekends. Floors must be swept and mopped daily. Towels, laundry bags, shoes, and jackets may remain out in the cell, but all other personal items,

THE FIRST MORNING

Getting used to life in prison is not easy. "I think the first morning is the toughest," recalled former inmate John Fuller, who served a ten-year sentence in federal prison for conspiracy to distribute cocaine. "No amount of reading or talking to ex-cons can help you wrap your mind around waking up to discover you've got a hard pillow under your head, a thick wool blanket replacing your goose-down comforter, and a gray ceiling a foot above your face. And it's not your favorite radio station that's awakened you—it's the . . . loudspeaker. I almost had a stroke the first time I had a jailhouse alarm go off next to my head. I woke up thinking an air-raid siren was going off."[2]

COUNTS

Prisoners are required to be in their cells during counts. Counts are times when prison staff count all prisoners. They are part of the daily routine in prison. In federal prisons, official counts normally take place at midnight, 3:00 a.m., 5:00 a.m., 4:00 p.m., and 9:00 p.m. If a prisoner fails to be in his cell during a count, he will face disciplinary actions.

such as calendars or posters, must be stored neatly in the inmate's locker.[3]

CELLIES

Getting used to cell life takes time. Part of that process is figuring out how to get along with a cellmate in such a small space. Unwritten rules among prisoners make this easier. While they may seem like common sense, these rules can mean the difference between peace and a fistfight. For example, hanging a sheet over the bunk to create privacy while a cellmate is using the toilet is a sign of respect. Don't comment on a cellmate's habits or read his mail. Never ask to borrow personal items such as toothpaste or deodorant.

For many new prisoners, meeting their cellmate, or *cellie*, is one of the most nerve-racking parts of prison. A compatible cellie can make the time spent in the cell tolerable. A disagreeable cellie can make a prisoner's time completely miserable.

Ron Self, who was serving a sentence at San Quentin for attempted murder, learned this the hard way. Self, who told his story on *Ear Hustle*, had a man called Duck as his first cellie. They lived together for six months. When Self first met Duck, it was a bad situation. Self recalled:

> *I hear [a door] pop open and that's the cell I'm going to, and the door opens all the way and it's Duck, the guy that's looking at me like he wants to kill me. No matter what I did in the cell, it was wrong. I mean, he would yell. He would scream. He threatened to kill me. I would sleep with my back to the wall and one eye open, if you would call what I did sleeping, and sometimes he would just get down out of the bed in the middle of the night screaming, acting like he's going to kill me. That one six-month period felt more like 60 years.*[4]

DISCUSSION STARTERS

- In order to maintain peace in close quarters, inmates follow many unwritten rules. Do you have any unwritten rules you follow at school or at home? What are they?
- Prisons also have many strict, formal rules. Why do you think those rules exist?
- Prison cellmates spend hours together in close quarters. How does an inmate's cellie affect his or her prison experience?

CHAPTER SEVEN

JOBS AND MONEY

Inmates do cleaning work at Deuel Vocational Institution in Tracy, California.

E very federal inmate who is physically and mentally able is expected to work seven hours each day. Their jobs are known as work assignments. The jobs serve two main purposes. First, jobs give inmates something to do during their days. Second, the work inmates do keeps the prison running smoothly by providing services. Prisons operate like small cities—they require all the same services that cities do, from garbage collection to carpentry.

An inmate's first work assignment is usually in whatever department happens to have an opening. These first assignments are usually the least desirable jobs and require a low level of skill. These jobs are also the lowest paying of all prison work. They usually include tasks such as cleaning

An inmate works in a garden at a South Carolina prison.

bathrooms, picking up litter on prison grounds, or working in the laundry facilities. Some kitchen work also falls into this category. That usually includes serving food or washing dishes.

Work assignments are not permanent. Inmates can request different jobs, though the requests are not always honored. Many inmates hope to get skilled work assignments. These jobs often require mastery of a trade, such as plumbing, welding, or carpentry. These jobs also have higher wages. If an inmate wants one of these jobs but does not have the skills, more experienced inmates or staff members serve as teachers. The best-paying and most desirable assignment is usually to work as a clerk. Clerks help the prison staff run different departments.

UNICOR INDUSTRIES

One of the most sought-after work assignments for federal prisoners is with Unicor Industries, also known as Federal Prison Industries. Unicor is a

JOB PERKS

Clerk jobs often offer perks to prisoners, and one of the best spots is as a prison librarian. "If you're lucky enough to work in the library, you'll get first crack at the new books," former inmate John Fuller wrote in his book *A Day in Prison.* "And you've got a way to fill the downtime while you're at work and it can be a great side hustle since plenty of inmates will barter stuff such as cigarettes and stamps in order to be the first to read a newspaper or do the crossword."[1]

government-owned company that employs inmates. The company's jobs give inmates meaningful work and useful skills. Depending on the Unicor facility a prisoner works in, he or she may learn any number of skills such as carpentry, accounting, metal finishing, or garment construction. When the inmates are released, these skills can make finding a job easier.

In 2017, Unicor operated 59 factories and three farms, all within prison grounds. These facilities employed more than 10,000 inmates.[2] They make a variety of products, such as military uniforms, electronics, office furniture, license plates, and mattresses. Unicor also offers a variety of services. Its employees provide computer-aided design, data entry, and call center staffing. The US government and its agencies are the largest purchasers of Unicor products and services.

SPENDING MONEY

All prison jobs pay much less than jobs outside of prison do. In 2017, federal prisoners made an

PRISON STRIKES

On August 21, 2018, Unicor employees in 17 states began three weeks of sit-ins and hunger strikes. The low pay and forced labor amounted to what prisoners and advocates called "modern slavery." This treatment is legal under the Thirteenth Amendment to the US Constitution. The amendment outlaws slavery, but it still allows for people to be punished for a crime by providing forced labor. And Unicor representatives say extra expenses—in terms of security—force them to pay low wages.[3]

average of 12 cents to 40 cents per hour.[4] Inmates who have Unicor jobs earn more. Their wages range between 23 cents and $1.15 per hour.[5] Comparatively, the federal minimum wage in 2018 was $7.25 per hour.[6]

Rather than being delivered through a paycheck, an inmate's wages go directly into a prison account. This is similar to a personal bank account, except it is run by the prison. If an inmate owes fines or restitution, a portion of each week's wages are applied to that debt. Friends and family members are allowed to add money to a prisoner's account. Usually this amount has a limit, depending on whether the inmate is at a state or federal prison.

Prisoners can spend the money in their accounts at the commissary, which is a small store inside the prison. Prisons usually have one day each week set aside for shopping. Inmates receive an inventory list of what is available for purchase, and they fill out a form indicating what they would like to buy. Then the items are delivered to their cells.

Commissaries sell everything from shower shoes and bars of soap to MP3 players and potato chips. Prisoners often buy commissary food because the food provided in prisons is notoriously bland, unhealthy, and served in small portions. Tuna, coffee, protein bars, and instant soup are top sellers at

SHOPPING LIST

Listed below are items and prices from a 2016 commissary inventory at a federal prison. Although the prices may seem standard, they are expensive to prisoners who make low wages. For a prisoner who makes 12 cents an hour, buying a bar of Dove soap would require more than 15 hours, or more than two full days, of work.[8]

- Beef ramen: $0.30
- Folgers coffee grounds: $4.70
- Dove soap: $1.90
- Colgate Total toothpaste: $4.25
- Combination lock: $6.50
- Playing cards: $2.55
- LED book light: $12.95
- Chunk tuna: $1.80
- Strawberry Pop-Tarts: $2.25
- Timex watch: $37.05

commissaries. So are brand-name hygiene items, such as toothpaste and shampoo. The prison does provide basic hygiene items, but if an inmate has a favorite brand-name product, that is often high on his or her commissary shopping list. In the nonfiction book *A Day in Prison*, inmate Damien D., whose last name was withheld, explains:

When you first get here, you should immediately buy your hygiene products and then always stay stocked up on them. Once you order your stuff, it can take up to two weeks before you get it, so if you run out of something you could be burnt for a while. If that happens, someone could lend you a bar of soap, but if they are caught it's an infraction. . . . Both parties in a transaction like that get in trouble, so it's best not even to ask a friend to risk it. Besides, you never want to be in debt to anyone, even if it's for something as small as a bar of soap.[7]

As with many things in prison, personal property is handled differently than in the outside world. Sharing personal property is against prison rules. If caught doing this, a prisoner can face discipline, such as losing telephone privileges.

KEEPING IT SAFE

The commissary shopping system was created to stop contraband from entering the prison. In the past, visitors could bring items as gifts to prisoners. But these gifts often hid contraband items such as cigarettes or drugs. For example, "Sometimes [visitors] will try to bring in a book," said Frank Leonbruno, an Ohio sheriff's office chief deputy. "But they'll drop liquid drugs onto a page and send their

An inmate receives his regular meal at a Massachusetts prison.

PRISON CURRENCY

Trading frequently happens in prisons, despite the policies against it. Inmates are not allowed to have cash, so they often create other types of currency. In many prisons, this currency is postage stamps. Inmates can purchase stamps legally at the commissary. But they are limited to a total of 40 stamps in their possession. Anything beyond that is considered contraband.

As a currency, stamps function the same way cash would outside of prison. For example, an inmate might offer 30 stamps to a library clerk to be the first person to complete a crossword puzzle in the daily newspaper. The library clerk can then trade those stamps for something he wants. In addition to stamps, inmates use other items as currency. This may include ramen noodles and cigarettes.

friend a letter telling them to suck on the top corner of page 10."[9] To prevent this type of contraband smuggling from happening, visitors are no longer allowed to bring gifts to prisoners. Instead, the commissaries offer items that have been cleared for safety by the prison.

Though commissary shopping has helped curb the contraband problem, inmates still find ways around this system. Prison staff members carefully track each inmate's purchases to make sure no one is stockpiling supplies and then reselling them. "If [an inmate] bought 20 cans of soup today and another 20 tomorrow, it would be confiscated," said Kathy Rose, an Ohio jail administrator. "We make sure they're not storing it or trading it with other inmates for any reason."[10]

It's not just trading that prison staff worry about when it comes to commissary goods. The goods can be used to make weapons. The most common of these are known as shanks or shivs. These weapons are any object that has been sharpened to a point. Prisoners make them out of a variety of readily available items—toothbrushes, plastic forks, can lids, and even hard candy. Prisoners make blunt objects to use as weapons, too. For example, they may put combination locks or soup cans into socks. Swinging the weighted sock during a fight can cause serious injuries.

DISCUSSION STARTERS

- Inmates earn an average of 12 cents to 40 cents per hour. Do you think these wages are fair?
- Do you think inmates should be required to work in prison?
- Prisoners are allowed to purchase a variety of items at the commissary. How does this benefit inmates? If commissaries did not exist, how would prison be different?

CHAPTER EIGHT

MIND, BODY, AND SPIRIT

Inmates practice yoga at Deschutes County Jail In Bend, Oregon.

Jonathan Chiu stood with a group of runners. "With a countdown—three, two, one—coach Frank Ruona announced, 'Go,' and more than 30 men started running around a half-dirt, half-asphalt track," recalled Chiu, who was serving a prison sentence for first-degree murder.[1] He and his fellow runners were participating in a prison marathon as part of the 1,000 Mile Club.

"It began like any other run in here, dodging large geese and other prisoners out for strolls," said Chiu. "We raced past concrete walls, barbed wire, and exercise areas, overlooked by armed correctional officers in watchtowers."[2] To complete the marathon, inmates had to run 105 laps around the prison

Inmates run in a marathon at Utah State Prison.

yard's track. As his miles added up, Chiu began to falter. An asthma attack restricted his breathing, and pain shot through his knees. "Barely conscious, and losing track of where I was, I told myself: 'Just keep going,'" recalled Chiu.[3] When he had only 12 laps left, an alarm sounded in the yard. It meant somewhere in the prison a disturbance was taking place. When this happens, all prisoners are required to sit down where they are and wait for the all clear.

At first, the alarm seemed like a lucky break—he would have time to recover from his asthma and knee pain. But it turned into something much bigger than that. "For a moment, I just lay on the ground staring up at the clear blue sky, feeling almost like I wasn't in prison anymore," said Chiu. After 30 minutes the prisoners received the all clear, and Chiu finished the marathon with a newfound sense of pride. "I want to do better, be better, be someone who doesn't give up anymore, running till the last lap. Running helps me feel pride and excitement inside what is essentially a storage room with a toilet, my cell, in a building with 800 different personalities," said Chiu.[4]

Chiu's participation in the prison marathon benefited him in a variety of ways. Training for it helped him to get physically fit. Wanting to finish the marathon gave him a goal to strive for. It gave him something positive to think about throughout the day. And when he finished the marathon, it made him feel good about himself. For inmates facing long sentences, this kind of activity that nurtures the mind, body, and spirit is what can make the time in prison bearable.

THE MIND

Day-to-day life in prison can become a dull series of cell time, meals, exercise, and strict social orders. The monotony can make many inmates depressed, discouraged, withdrawn, or even violent. One way prisoners take the edge off this daily grind is by finding ways to keep their minds healthy and active. Most prisoners find that visits from friends and family boost their mental health more than any other activity. Visiting rules vary from prison to prison, but they follow a basic pattern. One day each week is set aside as a day for an inmate to receive visitors.

Prison visits provide hope and support, and they've proved

STAYING IN TOUCH

In addition to in-person visits, there are several other ways that inmates can keep in touch with family and friends. In federal prisons, each inmate receives 300 minutes per month for phone calls. They may speak on the phone for a maximum of 15 minutes per call. Federal inmates also have access to a secured, monitored email system. It allows for email only—inmates do not have access to a web browser. Inmates may also send and receive letters through the mail.

to have lasting positive effects on inmates. A 2011 study showed inmates who received at least one visit at any time during their incarceration were less likely to commit another felony. And they were also less likely to violate the terms of their parole. "I think visitation has been largely viewed as a concession that's given to inmates," said Grant Duwe, director of the study. "I don't know if there has been a great deal of thought given to the public safety benefits that visitation might have."[5]

Another way inmates keep their minds active is through education. Prisons offer many educational opportunities. Any federal prisoner who does not have a high school diploma or a GED certificate must take 240 hours of literacy classes or earn a GED. Prisoners may also take a variety of other classes on topics ranging from parenting to personal health. A few college courses are also available, but the prisoners must pay for these themselves.

GOOD TIME CREDIT

Learning to balance the mind, body, and spirit is not easy. But behaving peacefully gives inmates a chance to earn good time credit. Good time credit is time reduced from a prisoner's sentence as a reward for good behavior. Federal inmates are eligible for 54 days of good time credit on the first anniversary of their incarceration and every year afterward. Good time credit can be accumulated over time. Acts of heroism, such as saving another person's life in the midst of violence, may result in a prisoner earning additional good time credit. Breaking prison rules can mean losing good time credit.

THE BODY

Staying physically fit is a top priority for many prisoners. Exercising allows them to burn off extra energy and reduces stress. Most prisons have what is known as a yard. It is a large outdoor space that usually has basketball courts, softball fields, and a running track. Prisons also have indoor exercise areas with treadmills and stationary bikes. Inmates can also take group fitness classes, such as yoga.

Maintaining a healthy body is important for inmates. Prisoners have a higher rate of diseases than the general public. Infectious diseases—those caused by bacteria, viruses, or fungi—are common among inmates due to close living quarters. Other chronic illnesses affect prisoners, too. High blood pressure, asthma, and arthritis are all common. Prisons have a legal responsibility to treat all of these conditions.

THE BENEFITS OF BOOKS

The need to fill long stretches of time or a desire to learn leads many inmates to the library. Books that could allude to criminal activities—for example, books that explain how to make bombs or weapons—are banned. But many other books are available. Eddie Parnell, an inmate serving time on a drug charge, explained the value of prison libraries. "A TV cost $275 and we made $30 a month working in the kitchen," Parnell said. "So I would just dig my heels into a good story. . . . Libraries reduce mental, emotional, and physical conflicts in the prison system. If a person is reading a book, they're not picking a fight in the next cell over."[6]

Prison doctors, nurses, and
dentists provide this care for
all inmates.

Another health problem
many inmates face is drug
addiction. Federal prisons offer
treatment programs to help
inmates break their addiction.
The most intensive program
is called the Residential Drug
Abuse Program. Prisoners live
in a special unit with other
inmates who are trying to break their addiction to drugs.
The program typically lasts nine months. This program
has resulted in less violence in prisons and lower rates
of recidivism.

PRISON GANGS

Not all prisoners find their place
in prison by exercising, studying,
or practicing religion. In the search
to find belonging and support
in prison, some inmates turn to
gangs. Gangs can serve as a form
of protection and power in prison.
Gangs determine the social order
in prison, such as which bathroom
a prisoner may use or which
table he sits at for meals. Gang
members stand up for one another
if the social order is disrespected
by another gang's member. This
often leads to fights, and the
majority of violence in prisons is
connected to gangs.

THE SPIRIT

Spiritual guidance also helps many inmates. Prisoners of
all faiths are guaranteed the right to practice their religion.
Most prisons have full-time chaplains to help inmates with
their spiritual needs. The chaplains hold religious services
each Sunday.

A TYPICAL DAY
IN PRISON

Prisons follow a strict daily schedule that maintains order. A loudspeaker or bell announces when prisoners may move from one area to another. This time is known as a ten-minute move. Each prison's schedule is a little different, based on security level. But most follow a pattern similar to the medium-security facility schedule outlined in the book *A Day in Prison* by John Fuller.[7]

5:00 a.m.	Optional morning prayer
5:30 a.m.	Lights on
6:00 a.m.	Breakfast
7:00 a.m.	Exercise, morning prayer, reading
7:30 a.m.	Shower
8:00 a.m.	Work
11:00 a.m.	Lunch
12:00 p.m.	Work
2:00 p.m.	Exercise, shower, laundry
3:00 p.m.	Visitation, self-help group, or college class
4:00 p.m.	Head count
4:30 p.m.	Dinner
5:00 p.m.	More education or therapy opportunities
6:00 p.m.	Phone time, socializing, watching TV
9:00 p.m.	Locked back in cell, reading, writing

Inmates relax and socialize at Jefferson County Detention Facility in Colorado.

A Catholic cardinal blesses inmates from Massachusetts Correctional Institution–Framingham.

Accommodating prisoners' faith takes many forms. For example, a Jewish prisoner who keeps kosher must follow a diet that has strict rules. For this reason, a prisoner is allowed to request a kosher meal. If the prison cannot provide one, the prisoner may be considered for transfer to another facility where it is available.

Allowing prisoners to practice their religions has resulted in decreased recidivism rates. Programs for prisoners of all faiths operate in prisons. One of the most successful is the InnerChange Freedom Initiative (IFI). It began operating in US prisons in 1997. This Christian organization provides reentry skills and faith-based support to inmates, such as how to get involved in a church upon release from prison. A 2003 study tracked the recidivism rates for people who participated in IFI. Those who completed the program were 60 percent less likely to return to prison within two years than their peers.[8]

DISCUSSION STARTERS

- Prisons offer many ways for inmates to exercise and stay physically fit. Why is this especially important in prisons? How would removing these options affect the prison population?

- Inmates receive education opportunities in prison. How does this benefit society? What effect might this have on a prisoner after release?

- Freedom to practice religion is guaranteed in prisons. What role might spirituality play in the daily lives of prisoners?

CHAPTER NINE

LEAVING
PRISON

Inmates take classes or go through programs to prepare for life after prison.

While the strict rules of prison life may feel limiting to inmates, they also provide a level of structure and stability. So, while inmates are eager to be released from prison, the idea of living without that structure and stability may seem daunting. Near the end of his 20-year sentence, inmate Jerry Metcalf explained:

> I'm told when to eat, when to sleep, when to go outside, when to talk with and see my family, when to shower, when to cut my hair or iron my clothes. My money is managed for me; I pay zero taxes; and my health care (what little there is of it) is free and monitored by others. I can't remember the last time I had to make a major decision like that for myself. I grow nervous just imagining the prospect.[1]

This anxiety is common for an inmate whose long sentence is nearing completion. Dreams of freedom in the outside world help many prisoners get through their years of incarceration. But, as release nears, the reality of life outside of prison weighs heavily on the minds of many inmates. They face huge challenges. Many are estranged from their families and friends after decades in prison. They may have few or no contacts in the outside world. When they leave prison, they have only their clothes, a bus ticket, and between $10 and

$200, depending on the state where they were incarcerated. With these meager resources, they must begin a new life.

A major challenge is figuring out how to live in a world that has changed immensely, especially regarding technology. Prisoners released after 20 or 30 years behind bars find the world has changed without them. Inmates who went into prison in the 1980s, for example, knew a world where people made calls on landlines and used tokens to ride the subway. After release, they had to figure out how to use smartphones and metro cards. The entire process can be overwhelming and disorienting.

RELEASE

Every year more than 500,000 prisoners are released nationwide.[2] Inmates may be released from prison in two ways: max out or go on parole. Maxing out means the prisoner has completed his maximum sentence. In the United States, more than one in five state prisoners max out.[3]

"IT'S GOING TO TAKE A MINUTE"

In 2015, Stanley Bailey was released from prison after serving more than 30 years. Even everyday events caught him off guard. When Bailey stood on a sidewalk next to a busy street for the first time since his release, he had to take a deep breath. "Yeah, this is going to take some getting used to," he said. He stepped back from the curb, toward the houses along the sidewalk, and scanned the road. "It's real uncomfortable. It's going to take a minute. I haven't had a car go by me in almost 30 years."[4]

They are released back into their communities without any supervision or support from the criminal justice system. They are left on their own to reestablish their lives. Some states offer reentry programs, but these services are not mandatory.

The second way a prisoner can be released is on parole. In this case, the prisoner still has time left on his sentence. But he is allowed to serve the remainder of the sentence outside of prison under certain conditions. The average length of parole is 19 months.[5]

The conditions of parole include many strict rules. A parolee must report in person to his parole officer regularly. He must follow all state and federal laws. He must have a job.

At the receiving and release area of a prison, inmates have to wait for their cases to be processed before they can be officially released.

A parolee cannot move without permission, and he cannot use drugs or alcohol. Sometimes a parolee has special terms in his parole, such as wearing a tracking device or attending drug counseling.

REENTRY PROGRAMS

Many released inmates fear failure. They do not want to go back to prison. Reentry programs have the goal of easing prisoners' transition back into society. These programs can take a number of forms.

In federal prisons, the Release Preparation Program begins for all inmates about 18 months before they're scheduled to be released. The program focuses on teaching inmates how to find and keep a job. Inmates practice job interviews and learn to write résumés. The goal is to help the inmates find jobs so they can fully support themselves once they're out of prison and living on their own.

RECIDIVISM RATES

Recidivism is a real risk for newly released prisoners. Data from the National Institute of Justice shows how serious the problem of recidivism is. It tracked inmates released from state prisons in 2005, and the findings showed:

- Two-thirds of prisoners are rearrested within three years of prison release.
- Three-quarters of prisoners are rearrested within five years of prison release.
- Offenders who commit property crimes—such as burglary, arson, or vandalism—were the most likely to be rearrested, with a rate of 82 percent. Drug offenders had a rearrest rate of 77 percent.[6]

Federal inmates nearing release may be sent to a residential reentry center (RRC) before their release date. RRCs are commonly referred to as halfway houses. They are closely supervised housing units. The amount of time a person spends in an RRC varies. On average, however, most RRCs house people for six months or 10 percent of their sentence—whichever amount of time is less.[7]

As in prison, people in RRCs must be present for daily counts and curfews. They cannot take drugs or alcohol. They cannot leave the property without signing out. However, people living in RRCs do have more freedom than prison inmates. They may leave for job interviews, work, medical appointments, or visits with friends and family.

The goal of RRC programs is to offer offenders guidance on how to reestablish their connections with the community. RRCs aim to lower recidivism rates by smoothing the transition from prison to society. RRCs provide resources and advice on how to find housing and jobs. Inmates are expected to find full-time jobs within 15 days of arriving at an RRC. In turn, inmates pay 25 percent of their wages to the RRC for their housing costs. This helps fund the program and also helps inmates get used to paying bills.

FINDING SUPPORT

While reentry programs aim to reduce recidivism, data

shows that even with the support of halfway houses, many

released inmates still struggle. A 2013 study in Pennsylvania

compared the first year of release for halfway house residents

with that of inmates who were released directly into the

community. Those who spent time in a halfway house before

being released in 2010 and 2011 still had a recidivism rate of

17.7 percent.[8]

High recidivism rates became
an issue in California when the
state reformed its Three Strikes
Law. This law first took effect in
1994, and it profoundly affected
people convicted there. It
required a mandatory increase in
prison time for repeat offenders.
Offenders with a second felony
conviction had to serve twice
the minimum amount of time
that had been required for
their crimes. Offenders with

WORK RELEASE PROGRAMS

Work release programs help
prisoners adjust to holding a
job before their release from
prison. Each state has different
standards, but in most cases,
prisoners are eligible for work
release when they have less than
a year left on their sentence.
In Minnesota, one work release
program is called Sentencing
to Serve (STS). Offenders in
the STS program go into the
community and perform jobs such
as maintaining public parks and
trails. The offenders are closely
supervised while in the community.
This experience provides a bridge
between incarceration and freedom,
with the goal that prisoners will
have an easier time returning to
life outside of prison.

a third felony conviction faced a minimum of 25 years to life in prison, no exceptions. In 2012, Californians voted to amend the law. With this reform, offenders sentenced under the Three Strikes Law could ask a judge to reduce their sentences. Over a few years, thousands of prisoners were released.[9] With few organized, easy-to-access resources, many released prisoners were left to fend for themselves. The result was a high rate of recidivism.

In an attempt to stop this, California writer Scott Budnick started the Anti-Recidivism Coalition (ARC) in 2013. ARC's goal was to provide mentors to newly released prisoners. The mentors advise former inmates on topics ranging from finances to education. The results have been impressive. There was a recidivism rate of less than 10 percent among the 450 former inmates who participated in the program. In comparison, California's general recidivism rate is nearly 60 percent.[10]

Though prisons have changed greatly throughout the nation's history, they still have a

MAJOR CHALLENGES

Most released prisoners want to return to their communities as law-abiding, productive citizens. They face many unique challenges as convicted felons, though. Having a job is the best predictor of a successful reentry. But finding a business willing to hire a convicted felon is not always easy. Between 60 and 75 percent of offenders cannot find a job within a year of release.[11] The same is true of finding housing. Many landlords are unwilling to rent to a convicted felon.

long way to go. The criminal justice system is still filled with racial bias, both in policing and in policies that put people of color at a disadvantage. The result of these policies is mass incarceration, with overcrowded prisons and poor living conditions for inmates. When a prisoner is released, he faces a high risk of being rearrested or being isolated within his community. But this can change. Many nonprofit groups are working to improve conditions for prisoners across the nation. And local, state, and federal lawmakers are fighting to change laws to make them more just.

DISCUSSION STARTERS

- Upon release, many inmates fear they may wind up back in prison. Why is recidivism a real possibility?
- What resources do prisoners have to support them when they reenter society?
- What do you think would be most difficult about reentering society after a prison sentence?

ESSENTIAL FACTS

SIGNIFICANT EVENTS

- During early American history, most people who broke the law faced consequences that involved public shaming and corporal punishment.

- The world's first modern prison—Eastern State Penitentiary in Pennsylvania—opened in the United States in 1829.

- Unrest resulting from the civil rights movement, the Vietnam War, and increased drug use led many citizens to demand that the country get tougher on crime in the 1960s.

KEY PLAYERS

- President Richard Nixon declared a War on Drugs in June 1971. He pushed the US criminal justice system to focus heavily on drug crime, including through instituting mandatory sentences for drug-related offenses.

- Under President Ronald Reagan, federal funding increased for the criminal justice system, and mandatory minimum sentences for drug offenses became legal in the 1980s, which led to more people being arrested and kept imprisoned for longer periods of time.

- US attorney general Loretta Lynch publicly identified problems in 2016 that women—especially mothers—faced in prison.

IMPACT ON SOCIETY

- In 2018, US jails and prisons held almost 2.3 million people.

- More than 2.7 million American children have a parent in prison.

- US taxpayers spend an average of $80 billion dollars per year on correctional facilities, from local jails to federal penitentiaries.

QUOTE

"I think most Americans have no idea of the scale and scope of mass incarceration in the United States. Unless you're directly impacted by the system, unless you have a loved one who's behind bars, unless you've done time yourself, unless you have a family member who's been branded a criminal and felon and can't get work, can't find housing, [is] denied even food stamps to survive, unless the system directly touches you, it's hard to even imagine that something of this scope and scale could even exist."

—*Michelle Alexander, writer, civil rights advocate, and lawyer*

GLOSSARY

acquittal
The act of setting free by declaring not guilty.

aggravated battery
Illegally touching another person with the intention to harm.

chaplain
A member of the clergy who performs religious or emotionally supportive duties for an institution.

commissary
A store that sells food and equipment.

contraband
Items that are banned.

corporal punishment
Any type of punishment that is done to a person's body, such as whipping or branding.

felony
A crime more serious than a misdemeanor, usually punishable by imprisonment.

forfeit
To give up something valuable as a consequence.

GED
A General Education Development certificate, which proves a person's high school–level education.

grant
A gift of money intended for a certain purpose, such as college tuition.

incarceration
To be imprisoned.

initiative
An act or strategy intended to resolve a difficulty or improve a situation.

mandatory minimum sentence
The shortest amount of time a person convicted of a crime must serve, as required by law.

manslaughter
An unlawful killing of a person by impulse or without planning.

misdemeanor
A crime with less serious penalties than those assessed for a felony.

parole
Early release from prison because of good behavior under the condition that good behavior continue.

penitentiary
A prison.

probation
The release of a prisoner who remains under supervision instead of incarceration.

punitive
Intended to punish.

recidivism
Falling again into crime; returning to prison.

rehabilitate
To use education or therapy to return someone to a normal life after criminal activity or substance abuse.

restitution
Money paid for injury or loss.

traffic
To deal and trade in something, often something illegal.

ADDITIONAL RESOURCES

SELECTED BIBLIOGRAPHY

Fuller, John. *A Day in Prison*. Skyhorse, 2017.

Morris, Norval, and David J. Rothman. *The Oxford History of the Prison: The Practice of Punishment in Western Society*. Oxford UP, 1995.

"Trends in U.S. Corrections." *Sentencing Project*, 22 June 2018, sentencingproject.org. Accessed 19 Oct. 2018.

Wagner, Peter, and Wendy Sawyer. "Mass Incarceration: The Whole Pie 2018." *Prison Policy Initiative*, 14 Mar. 2018, prisonpolicy.org. Accessed 19 Oct. 2018.

FURTHER READINGS

Berne, Emma Carlson. *World's Scariest Prisons*. Scholastic, 2014.

Burling, Alexis. *Race in the Criminal Justice System*. Abdo, 2018.

Goozh, Judi, and Sue Jeweler. *Tell Me about When Moms and Dads Come Home from Jail*. Jessica Kingsley Publishers, 2018.

ONLINE RESOURCES

Booklinks
NONFICTION NETWORK
FREE! ONLINE NONFICTION RESOURCES

To learn more about the US prison system and prison life, visit **abdobooklinks.com** or scan this QR code. These links are routinely monitored and updated to provide the most current information available.

MORE INFORMATION

For more information on this subject, contact or visit the following organizations:

Federal Bureau of Prisons

320 First St. NW
Washington, DC 20534
202-307-3198
bop.gov

The Federal Bureau of Prisons is the US government agency charged with the custody and care of federal inmates. Its site provides information about the facilities, inmates, and staff that make up the federal prison system.

The Marshall Project

156 West Fifty-Sixth St., Suite 701
New York, NY 10019
212-803-5200
themarshallproject.org

The Marshall Project is a nonprofit news source dedicated to the criminal justice system. Among its many columns is one called Life Inside, which is written by inmates describing their experiences in prison.

The Sentencing Project

1705 DeSales St. NW, Eighth Floor
Washington, DC 20036
202-628-0871
sentencingproject.org

The Sentencing Project is a nonprofit organization dedicated to working toward a more fair and effective criminal justice system. Its site includes original research, current prison data, and campaigns for criminal justice reforms.

SOURCE NOTES

CHAPTER 1. A CULTURE SHOCK

1. "Left Behind." *Ear Hustle*, episode 8, 27 Sept. 2017, earhustlesq.com. Podcast audio 12:05. Accessed 14 Jan. 2019.

2. "United States of America." *World Prison Brief*, 2016, prisonstudies.org. Accessed 14 Jan. 2019.

3. Michelle Ye Hee Lee. "Does the United States Really Have 5 Percent of the World's Population and One Quarter of the World's Prisoners?" *Washington Post*, 30 Apr. 2015, washingtonpost.com. Accessed 14 Jan. 2019.

4. "Statistical Report (SB601)." *San Quentin State Prison*, 11 Nov. 2018, cdcr.ca.gov. Accessed 14 Jan. 2019.

5. Peter Wagner and Bernadette Rabuy. "Following the Money of Mass Incarceration." *Prison Policy Initiative*, 25 Jan. 2017, prisonpolicy.org. Accessed 14 Jan. 2019.

6. "A Shared Sentence." *Anne E. Casey Foundation*, Apr. 2016, aecf.org. Accessed 14 Jan. 2019.

7. Peter Wagner and Wendy Sawyer. "Mass Incarceration: The Whole Pie 2018." *Prison Policy Initiative*, 14 Mar. 2018, prisonpolicy.org. Accessed 14 Jan. 2019.

8. Wagner and Sawyer, "Mass Incarceration: The Whole Pie 2018."

9. Wagner and Sawyer, "Mass Incarceration: The Whole Pie 2018."

10. Wagner and Sawyer, "Mass Incarceration: The Whole Pie 2018."

11. "About Our Facilities." *Federal Bureau of Prisons*, n.d., bop.gov. Accessed 14 Jan. 2019.

12. Wagner and Sawyer, "Mass Incarceration: The Whole Pie 2018."

13. "Understanding Security Levels." *Zoukis Prisoner Resources*, n.d., prisonerresource.com. Accessed 14 Jan. 2019.

14. "Prison Security Levels." *Federal Bureau of Prisons*, 24 Nov. 2018, bop.gov. Accessed 14 Jan. 2019.

15. "Understanding Security Levels."

16. "Understanding Security Levels."

17. Ray Sanchez and Alexandra Field. "What's Life Like in Supermax Prison?" *CNN*, 25 June 2015, cnn.com. Accessed 14 Jan. 2019.

CHAPTER 2. THE HISTORY OF AMERICAN PRISONS

1. Charles Dickens. *American Notes*. London: Chapman & Hall, 1842. *Project Gutenberg*. Accessed 14 Jan. 2019.

2. Norval Morris and David J. Rothman, eds. *The Oxford History of the Prison*. Oxford UP, 1998. 116.

3. Lawrence M. Friedman. *Crime and Punishment in American History*. Harper, 1993. 262.

4. Friedman, *Crime and Punishment in American History*, 267.

5. Peter Wagner and Wendy Sawyer. "States of Incarceration: The Global Context 2018." *Prison Policy Initiative*, June 2018, prisonpolicy.org. Accessed 14 Jan. 2019.

6. Adam Gopnik. "How We Misunderstand Mass Incarceration." *New Yorker*, 10 Apr. 2017, newyorker.com. Accessed 14 Jan. 2019.

CHAPTER 3. MASS INCARCERATION

1. Sarah Childress. "Michelle Alexander: 'A System of Racial and Social Control.'" *Frontline: Locked Up in America—The Prison State*, 29 Apr. 2014, pbs.org. Accessed 14 Jan. 2019.

2. Richard Gunderman. "The Incarceration Epidemic." *Atlantic*, 20 June 2013, theatlantic.com. Accessed 14 Jan. 2019.

3. Michael W. Flamm. *Law and Order*. Columbia UP, 2005. 1.

4. "A Brief History of the Drug War." *Drug Policy Alliance*, n.d., drugpolicy.org. Accessed 14 Jan. 2019.

5. "A Brief History of the Drug War."

6. "Trends in U.S. Corrections." *US Sentencing Project*, June 2018. sentencingproject.org. Accessed 14 Jan. 2019.

7. Peter Wagner and Wendy Sawyer. "Mass Incarceration: The Whole Pie 2018." *Prison Policy Initiative*, 14 Mar. 2018, prisonpolicy.org. Accessed 14 Jan. 2019.

8. Keely Herring. "Was a Prison Built Every 10 Days to House a Fast-Growing Population of Nonviolent Inmates?" *PolitiFact*, 31 July 2015, politifact.com. Accessed 14 Jan. 2019.

9. "Prison Spending in 2015." *Vera: The Price of Prisons*, n.d., vera.org. Accessed 14 Jan. 2019.

10. US Bureau of the Census. "Real Median Personal Income in the United States." *Federal Reserve Bank of Saint Louis, Economic Research, FRED Economic Data*, n.d., fred.stlouisfed.org. Accessed 14 Jan. 2019.

11. "At $75,560, Housing a Prisoner in California Now Costs More Than a Year at Harvard." *Los Angeles Times*, 4 June 2017, latimes.com. Accessed 14 Jan. 2019.

12. "Prison Spending in 2015."

13. Matt Ford. "The Everyday Struggle of a Child Whose Parents Are Incarcerated." *Smithsonian*, Jan. 2017, smithsonianmag.com. Accessed 14 Jan. 2019.

CHAPTER 4. RACE AND PRISON

1. Leah Sakala. "Breaking Down Mass Incarceration in the 2010 Census." *Prison Policy Initiative*, 28 May 2014, prisonpolicy.org. Accessed 14 Jan. 2019.

2. Cara Buckley. "Ava DuVernay on Modern Slavery in America." *New York Times*, 5 Oct. 2016, newyorktimes.com. Accessed 14 Jan. 2019.

3. Sarah Childress. "Michelle Alexander: 'A System of Racial and Social Control.'" *Frontline: Locked Up in America—The Prison State*, 29 Apr. 2014, pbs.org. Accessed 14 Jan. 2019.

4. Patrick Sharkey. "Neighborhoods and the Black-White Mobility Gap." *Pew Charitable Trusts*, July 2009, pewtrusts.org. Accessed 14 Jan. 2019.

5. Bernadette Rabuy and Daniel Kopf. "Prisons of Poverty." *Prison Policy Initiative*, 9 July 2015, prisonpolicy.org. Accessed 14 Jan. 2019.

6. "Herstory." *Black Lives Matter*, n.d., blacklivesmatter.com. Accessed 14 Jan. 2019.

7. "Prison State." *Frontline*, season 2, episode 10, 29 Apr. 2014, *pbs.org*. 9:48. Accessed 14 Jan. 2019.

8. "How a Theory of Crime and Policing Was Born, and Went Terribly Wrong." *NPR*, 1 Nov. 2016, npr.org. Accessed 14 Jan. 2019.

9. "Stop and Frisk—The Human Impact." *Center for Constitutional Rights*, 26 July 2012, ccrjustice.org. Accessed 14 Jan. 2019.

10. Janell Ross. "There's a Lot of Chatter about 'Stop and Frisk.' Here Are the Facts." *Washington Post*, 5 Oct. 2016, washingtonpost.com. Accessed 14 Jan. 2019.

11. "Stop and Frisk—The Human Impact."

12. "Prison Is a Real-Life Example of the World White Supremacists Want." *Marshall Project*, 24 Aug. 2017, themarshallproject.com. Accessed 14 Jan. 2019.

13. Nazgol Ghandnoosh. "Black Lives Matter: Eliminating Racial Inequality in the Criminal Justice System." *Sentencing Project*, 2015, sentencingproject.org. Accessed 14 Jan. 2019.

CHAPTER 5. WOMEN IN PRISON

1. Wendy Sawyer. "The Gender Divide." *Prison Policy Initiative*, 9 Jan. 2018, prisonpolicy.org. Accessed 14 Jan. 2019.

2. Sawyer, "The Gender Divide."

3. Elizabeth Swavola, Kristine Riley, and Ram Subramanian. "Overlooked: Women and Jails in an Era of Reform." *Vera Institute of Justice*, 17 Aug. 2016, safetyandjusticechallenge.org. Accessed 14 Jan. 2019.

4. Duchess Harris. "Incarcerated Motherhood." *Journal of Race, Gender, and Ethnicity* vol. 6, issue 1, 2012–2013. *tourolaw.edu*. Accessed 14 Jan. 2019.

5. Melissa Jeltsen. "Women in Jail Are Fastest Growing Segment of America's Incarcerated Population." *Huffington Post*, 17 Aug. 2016, huffingtonpost.com. Accessed 14 Jan. 2019.

6. Swavola, Riley, and Subramanian, "Overlooked: Women and Jails in an Era of Reform."

7. Rebecca Project for Human Rights. "Mothers behind Bars." *National Women's Law Center*, 2010, nwlc.org. Accessed 14 Jan. 2019.

8. "Attorney General Loretta E. Lynch Delivers Remarks at the White House Women and the Criminal Justice System Convening." *US Department of Justice*, 30 Mar. 2016, justice.gov. Accessed 14 Jan. 2019.

9. Morgan Greene. "Number of Moms in US Prisons on the Rise." *Chicago Tribune*, 11 May 2018, chicagotribune.com. Accessed 14 Jan. 2019.

10. Aleks Kajstura. "Women's Mass Incarceration: The Whole Pie 2017." *Prison Policy Initiative*, 19 Oct. 2017, prisonpolicy.org. Accessed 14 Jan. 2019.

11. Harris, "Incarcerated Motherhood."

12. Kajstura, "Women's Mass Incarceration: The Whole Pie 2017."

13. Lydia O'Connor. "Federal Prisons Made Menstrual Products Free. Now Some States May Follow Suit." *Huffington Post*, 7 Feb. 2018, huffingtonpost.com. Accessed 14 Jan. 2019.

14. Wendy Sawyer. "Bailing Moms Out for Mother's Day." *Prison Policy Initiative*, 8 May 2017, prisonpolicy.org. Accessed 14 Jan. 2019.

15. Justin Jouvenal. "Raising Babies behind Bars." *Washington Post*, 11 May 2018, washingtonpost.com. Accessed 14 Jan. 2019.

16. Jouvenal, "Raising Babies behind Bars."

CHAPTER 6. THE FIRST DAYS IN PRISON

1. "Cellies." *Ear Hustle*, episode 1, 14 June 2017, earhustlesq.com. Podcast audio 4:38. Accessed 14 Jan. 2019.

2. John Fuller. *A Day in Prison*. Skyhorse, 2017. 3.

3. "Inmate Information Handbook, Federal Bureau of Prisons." *MCFP Springfield, MO*, Nov. 2012, bop.gov. Accessed 14 Jan. 2019.

4. "Cellies."

CHAPTER 7. JOBS AND MONEY

1. John Fuller. *A Day in Prison*. Skyhorse, 2017. 79–80.

2. "2017 Annual Report." *Unicor*, n.d., unicor.gov. Accessed 14 Jan. 2019.

3. German Lopez. "America's Prisoners Are Going on Strike in at Least 17 States." *Vox*, 22 Aug. 2018, vox.com. Accessed 14 Jan. 2019.

4. "Custody & Care: Work Programs." Bureau of Federal Prisons, n.d., bop.gov. Accessed 14 Jan. 2019.

5. "FPI General Overview Frequently Asked Questions." *Unicor*, n.d., unicor.gov. Accessed 14 Jan. 2019.

6. "Fair Labor Standards Act Advisor: What Is the Minimum Wage?" *US Department of Labor*, n.d., webapps.dol.gov. Accessed 14 Jan. 2019.

7. Fuller, *A Day in Prison*, 79–80.

8. "Federal Bureau of Prisons, TRUFACS, Commissary Shopping List." *Federal Bureau of Prisons*, 23 Feb. 2016, bop.gov. Accessed 14 Jan. 2019.

9. Max Reinhart. "What Can Inmates Buy in Jail?" *News-Herald*, 5 Aug. 2012, news-herald.com. Accessed 14 Jan. 2019.

10. Reinhart, "What Can Inmates Buy in Jail?"

CHAPTER 8. MIND, BODY, AND SPIRIT

1. Jonathan Chiu. "Marathon Man." *Marshall Project*, 11 May 2017, themarshallproject.com. Accessed 14 Jan. 2019.

2. Chiu, "Marathon Man."

3. Chiu, "Marathon Man."

4. Chiu, "Marathon Man."

5. John Rudolf. "Prison Visits Make Inmates Less Likely to Commit Crimes after Release, Study Finds." *Huffington Post*, 7 Dec. 2011, huffingtonpost.com. Accessed 14 Jan. 2019.

6. Jake Rossen. "Cell Service: Inside the World of Prison Librarians." *Mental Floss*, 11 Jan. 2018, mentalfloss.com. Accessed 14 Jan. 2019.

7. John Fuller. *A Day in Prison*. Skyhorse, 2017. xvi–xvii.

8. "InnerChange Freedom Initiative." Prison Fellowship, n.d., prisonfellowship.org. Accessed 14 Jan. 2019.

CHAPTER 9. LEAVING PRISON

1. Jerry Metcalf "The Everyday Chaos of Incarceration." *Marshall Project*, 1 Mar. 2018, themarshallproject.org. Accessed 14 Jan. 2019.

2. Katie Galloway and Kelly Duane de la Vega. "A Ride Home from Prison." *New York Times Op-Docs Video*, 16 July 2015, newyorktimes.com. 7:27. Accessed 14 Jan. 2019.

3. "Max Out: The Rise in Prison Inmates Released without Supervision." *Pew Charitable Trusts*, 4 June 2014, pewtrusts.org. Accessed 14 Jan. 2019.

4. Galloway and Duane de la Vega, "A Ride Home from Prison," 5:07.

5. "Probation and Parole Requirements." *Prison Fellowship*, n.d., prisonfellowship.org. Accessed 14 Jan. 2019.

6. Devah Pager and Bruce Western. "Investigating Prisoner Reentry." *National Institute of Justice Grant: Final Report*, Oct. 2009, ncjrs.gov. Accessed 14 Jan. 2019.

7. "Frequently Asked Questions about Federal Halfway Houses & Home Confinement." *Families Against Mandatory Minimums (FAMM)*, n.d., famm.org. Accessed 14 Jan. 2019.

8. "Recidivism Report 2013." *Pennsylvania Department of Corrections*, 8 Feb. 2013, nationalcia.org. Accessed 14 Jan. 2019.

9. Jon Mooallem. "You Just Got Out of Prison. Now What?" *New York Times Magazine*, 16 July 2015, nytimes.com. Accessed 14 Jan. 2019.

10. "The Coalition Today." *Anti-Recidivism Coalition (ARC)*, n.d., antirecidivism.org. Accessed 14 Jan. 2019.

11. "Recidivism." National Institute of Justice, 17 June 2014, nij.gov. Accessed 14 Jan. 2019.

INDEX

ABOUT THE AUTHORS

DUCHESS HARRIS, JD, PHD

Dr. Harris is a professor of American Studies at Macalester College and curator of the Duchess Harris Collection of ABDO books. She is also the coauthor of the titles in the collection, which features popular selections such as *Hidden Human Computers: The Black Women of NASA* and series including News Literacy and Being Female in America.

Before working with ABDO, Dr. Harris authored several other books on the topics of race, culture, and American history. She served as an associate editor for *Litigation News*, the American Bar Association Section of Litigation's quarterly flagship publication, and was the first editor in chief of *Law Raza*, an interactive online journal covering race and the law, published at William Mitchell College of Law. She has earned a PhD in American Studies from the University of Minnesota and a JD from William Mitchell College of Law.

KATE CONLEY

Kate Conley has been writing nonfiction books for children for more than a decade. When she's not writing, Conley spends her time reading, drawing, and solving crossword puzzles. She lives in Minnesota with her husband and two children.